The Forward book of poetry
2010

The Forward book of poetry

2010

FORWARD

LONDON

First published in Great Britain by
Forward Ltd · 84–86 Regent Street · London W1B 5DD
in association with
Faber and Faber · 3 Queen Square · London WC1N 3AU

ISBN 978 0 571 25363 0 (paperback)

Printed by Fulmar Colour Printing Company Limited, Croydon, UK

Mixed Sources
Product group from well-managed
forests and other controlled sources
www.fsc.org Cert no. TT-COC-002341
© 1996 Forest Stewardship Council
FSC

A CIP catalogue reference for this book
is available at the British Library.

To Michael Dineen. In memoriam

Contents

Shortlisted Poems – The Forward Prize for Best Collection

Shortlisted Poems – The Felix Dennis Prize for Best First Collection

Shortlisted Poems – The Forward Prize for Best Single Poem

Highly Commended Poems 2009

Preface

THE POWER OF THE WORD has always fascinated me, and especially the emotional complicity that exists between the word and the reader. It was this fascination that drove me to found Forward, the company behind the Forward Poetry Prizes, in 1985.

Words affect us, as readers, in extraordinary ways: they can move us to tears or laughter, offer consolation or make us incandescent with rage. The power of the word was the guiding principle for Forward from the start; and of course it also inspired the Forward Poetry Prizes, which we launched in 1991, for poets know the power of the word perhaps more intimately than anyone else.

This power was keenly felt by our 2009 judges – Tishani Doshi, David Harsent, Jean Sprackland and Nicholas Wroe, with Josephine Hart ably piloting their progress. Their passion for the poems they have chosen for this year's shortlist deserves its own celebration, as does the generous continuing support of our sponsors: Felix Dennis; Nick McDowell and Arts Council England; Faber and Faber; the Colman Getty team, including Dotti Irving, Liz Sich, Kate Wright-Morris and Truda Spruyt; and at Forward, the inimitable team of Will Scott, Lucy Naylor, Casey Jones and Christopher Stocks.

But in the end, of course, *The Forward book of poetry* is really a celebration of the poets themselves, and the mysterious and (to me at least) magical way that poetry can affect us. I hope you enjoy reading this year's poems as much as I have.

William Sieghart

Foreword

POETRY IS 'ONE PERSON TALKING TO ANOTHER' according to TS Eliot. My
fellow judges – Tishani Doshi, David Harsent, Jean Sprackland (each a
prizewinning poet) and the acclaimed journalist Nicholas Wroe – and
myself were privileged to 'listen' to the individual voice of many poets.
Since poetic sensibility often rests at the edge of experience it requires
of the reader a particular intensity of concentration. We were richly
rewarded by poems that were sometimes inspired by the great life
experiences – love, loss, birth and death – and sometimes by a
momentary floating image or insight. Many lines not only echoed in our
minds but indeed in many cases took up residence there. This is the
triumph of poetry. It is the highest of the literary art forms. It is also the
most demanding as it can force the choice between 'perfection of the
work rather than of the life' in Yeats's telling phrase. All of us on the
judging panel are only too aware of the profound dedication that went
into each collection, whether it was shortlisted or not. We wish to thank
all the poets on the longlists and to express our admiration.

For this year's *Forward book of poetry* we have selected for publication
two poems from each of the six shortlisted collections in the Best
Collection and Best First Collection categories, six poems shortlisted in
the Best Single Poem category, and a further selection of Highly (often
passionately) Commended poems from our individual longlists. We
hope that within this anthology you too will find many poems, or simply
lines from poems, that will meet Larkin's challenge that poetry should
help us to either 'enjoy or endure'.

'Whole skies of stars / are a lesser wonder / than all your lights at
evening, / all your lives. / When the lights go out I'm there, / moving on'
are haunting lines from Glyn Maxwell's 'Lit Windows', from *Hide Now*.
They illuminate the presence of the spectral 'watcher' who inhabits
many of his poems in this time sequence. Sharon Olds's work in
'One Secret Thing' has a tough, often shocking physicality. Her
'Self-Exam' – 'They tell you it won't make much sense, at first, / you
will have to learn the terrain' – describes a woman's precautionary
monthly examination of her breasts as dispassionately as an astronaut
might describe extraterrestrial planes. In her poem 'Diagnosis', the
disturbing, impossible self-awareness of the baby is equally unsettling.

Don Patterson's child in 'The Lie' from his collection *Rain* is 'a boy of maybe three or four. / His straps and chains were all the things he wore'. Lines from the title poem itself, 'Rain', *'forget the ink, the milk, the blood – / all was washed clean with the flood / we rose up from the falling waters / the fallen rain's own sons and daughters / and none of this, none of this matters'* are masterly in their rhythms. Patterson, poet and jazz musician, reminds us of Larkin's belief that jazz is as close to the unconscious as we can get.

Peter Porter takes the long perspective in his provocatively titled collection *Better Than God*. 'We, the holders of Philosophy's new Bibles, / look away from everything we know corrodes, and speak / Pentecostally if cautiously of the Plan of Man,' he tells us in his poem 'No Heaven Cold Enough' (Mr Porter's titles are a joy in themselves). Poetry begins in delight and ends in wisdom, Frost believed, though perhaps, as in Porter's 'Shakespeare's Defeat', 'no element / may carry life's prefigured comical audacity / Beyond its blood-veiled site'.

Christopher Reid's *A Scattering* is a Hardyesque sequence of poems dedicated to the 'woman much missed', his actress wife Lucinda who died in 2005. Grief, which has inspired some of our greatest poetry – Tennyson's *In Memoriam*, Milton's *Lycidas* – is also potentially dangerous territory for the writer. These poems however are always within Christopher Reid's artistic control – austere and dignified with occasional lines of almost weary wit. In 'Afterlife' he tells us, 'As if she couldn't bear not to be busy and useful / after her death, she willed her body to medical science'. As he passes the hospital… 'My wife is in there, somewhere, doing practical work'. Then the Frostian last line, 'I had work to do, too, in a different part of town'.

The celebration of the dead when 'the dead' are one's parents as is the case in Hugo Williams's 'West End Final' marks out quite another territory. His mother – also an actress – was celebrated by, amongst others, Cole Porter. 'You're the top, you're an ocean liner / You're the top, you're Margaret Vyner'. Williams's pen portrait, 'Poems to my Mother', culminates in the triumphant 'i.m. MV': 'You hurled yourself in the air / You dived on the ocean floor / You came to the end of your breath / You wound yourself into shore'.

The publication of a first collection is a seminal moment for a poet so our Best First Collection shortlist bears a special significance to those selected. Those poets not shortlisted should draw comfort from the fact that it was a truly close-run thing and also that the history of literature endlessly proves judges to be wrong.

From *Missing* by Siân Hughes we chose 'Sleep Training' and 'The Send Off', her already justly praised poem about the death of a baby. 'You don't even need to close your eyes. / They were born that way sealed shut. / You're a hard lesson to learn / Soft though you are and transparent'. Her poetry is rock-crystal hard, unsentimental and unforgettable. The poems in *The Striped World* by Emma Jones are both elliptical and visionary – in a parallel world of strange disjointed images within which we nevertheless find echoes of familiar experience. In 'Literary History' candles throw out 'inappropriate shadows / You can't be gothic before gothic *was* / You know, and Mary Wollenstonecraft / Hasn't given birth to Mary Shelley yet'.

In 'Natural Mechanical' by J O Morgan we meet Rocky, a dyslexic child on the Isle of Skye. He is a kind of reverse *enfant sauvage* who gives up on school where the letters of words 'are glue'. From then on 'His teaching to be gathered from the earth. / From scrub and thicket: profit, never dearth'. The entire book could as easily be titled *Birth of a Naturalist*. Lorraine Mariner's *Furniture* contains poems which have a literary speed-camera velocity, catching the moment and, crucially, the unexpected image in the picture – which, like Barthes' punctum, subtly distorts and to great effect. 'At school I always wanted to get injured': the opening line of 'Injured' is compelling. It continues with Holden Caulfield-like echoes with a wish for '…a serious illness / say diabetes (like my oldest friend Nicola's dad)'.

In Meirion Jordan's poem 'Calculus' from his collection *Moonrise*, the speaker tells us (warns us?) 'I will be here 'til the beachcombers are gone, / the massive sun washed up on the horizon… / I will be out late, then very late, / turning my pebbles at the spinning moon'. We are on high-alert in these poems. His 'Cry Wolf' tells of some long-distant past when poets 'go out like ghosts through the woods… / It's safer now. Nobody / loses an eye or a hand / to metaphor these days'.

Meghan O'Rourke's poem 'Descent' from her book *Half Life* has a language 'speed' all of its own. 'I was born a bastard in an amphetamine spree, / lit through with a mother's quickenings, / burrowing into her, afraid she would not have me, / and she would not have me'. Dream-like images of the river Styx – the word playfully inverted – are less *momento mori* than an Elizabeth Smart-like warning to look again.

In The Best Single Poem category we shortlisted Paul Farley's 'Moles', Michael Longley's 'Visiting Stanley Kunitz', Robert Robinson's 'At Roane Head', Elizabeth Speller's 'Finistère', George Szirtes's 'Song' and C K Williams's 'Either / Or'. These poems were selected after much consideration from more than 100 single poems. Each elicited a sudden delight that earned them their place on the list. The extraordinarily high number of submissions in all categories – 120 Best Collections, 60 Best First Collections – bears eloquent testimony to the pre-eminence of The Forward Prizes. A profound debt of gratitude is owed to its founder William Sieghart. The deep commitment of the judges to the art form of poetry led naturally to intense discussion and then, perhaps surprisingly, to a happy consensus. I greatly look forward to talking to my co-judges in October when from the six shortlisted in each category we will, with equal care and not a little humility, make our final choice.

Josephine Hart, *August* 2009.

Shortlisted Poems
The Forward Prize for Best Collection

Glyn Maxwell

EMPIRE STATE

Departed I could see her
from my new room in Manhattan,
lonely among letters
in the tallest word in English.

It's like she'd crept alongside,
a great bejewelled someone
at the dark edge of a party
we could not stand any longer.

And still at the wide window
we considered making contact,
she haplessly three-coloured
and I knowing all about that,

but we settled for the vista
through the traffic to the water.
Since *nothing lasts forever*
was about all I could muster.

Lit Windows

When I go home again,
when I know so many homes, but I mean the home
with the longest vowel, when I wander the old realm,
I pass them on the lane,
    boys turned to men,

so I turn back to a boy
to pass them saying nothing. For it's death
to be where one is not, where every breath
is a heaving of the oars
    alone at sea.

I could grow white and old
and I will, I am well aware, grow white and old
looking through lit windows of the world
for people in their rooms;
    for the blue, cold

light of a TV on
in an empty room... girl at a light so bright
she's silhouette... a man who hangs his coat
and stands quite still... a mother
    agrees with someone

over cake... the frosted light
of suppertime, of bathtime, of sex.
I don't have what I have from reading books
but stopping by your homes
    to see these sights

and wondering forever
who is someone else? Who on earth
are all these people to have known this with,
this world? Whole skies of stars
    are a lesser wonder

than all your lights at evening,
all your lives. When the lights go out I'm there,
moving on. When it's dark the stars are clear,
their immaterial eyes
    believing, disbelieving.

Sharon Olds

SELF-EXAM

They tell you it won't make much sense, at first,
you will have to learn the terrain. They tell you this
at thirty, and fifty, and some are late
beginners, at last lying down and walking
the bright earth of the breasts – the rounded,
cobbled, ploughed field of one,
with a listening walking, and then the other –
fingertip-stepping, divining, north
to south, east to west, sectioning
the low, fallen hills, sweeping
for mines. And the matter feels primordial,
unimaginable – dense,
cystic, phthistic, each breast like the innards
of a cell, its contents shifting and changing,
streambed gravel under walking feet, it
seems almost unpicturable, not
immemorial, but nearly un-
memorizable, but one marches,
slowly, through grave or fatal danger,
or no danger, one feels around in the
two tackroom drawers, ribs and
knots like leather bridles and plaited
harnesses and bits and reins,
one runs one's hands through the mortal tackle
in a jumble, in the dark, indoors. Outside –
night, in which these glossy ones were
ridden to a froth of starlight, bareback.

Diagnosis

By the time I was six months old, she knew something
was wrong with me. I got looks on my face
she had not seen on any child
in the family, or the extended family,
or the neighborhood. My mother took me in
to the pediatrician with the kind hands,
a doctor with a name like a suit size for a wheel:
Hub Long. My mom did not tell him
what she thought in truth, that I was Possessed.
It was just these strange looks on my face –
he held me, and conversed with me,
chatting as one does with a baby, and my mother
said, She's doing it now! Look!
She's doing it now! and the doctor said,
What your daughter has
is called a sense
of humor. Ohhh, she said, and took me
back to the house where that sense would be tested
and found to be incurable.

Don Paterson

The Lie

As was my custom, I'd risen a full hour
before the house had woken to make sure
that everything was in order with The Lie,
his drip changed and his shackles all secure.

I was by then so practised in this chore
I'd counted maybe thirteen years or more
since last I'd felt the urge to meet his eye.
Such, I liked to think, was our rapport.

I was at full stretch to test some ligature
when I must have caught a ragged thread, and tore
his gag away; though as he made no cry,
I kept on with my checking as before.

Why do you call me The Lie? he said. I swore:
it was a child's voice. I looked up from the floor.
The dark had turned his eyes to milk and sky
and his arms and legs were all one scarlet sore.

He was a boy of maybe three or four.
His straps and chains were all the things he wore.
Knowing I could make him no reply
I took the gag before he could say more

and put it back as tight as it would tie
and locked the door and locked the door and locked the door

RAIN

I love all films that start with rain:
rain, braiding a windowpane
or darkening a hung-out dress
or streaming down her upturned face;

one big thundering downpour
right through the empty script and score
before the act, before the blame,
before the lens pulls through the frame

to where the woman sits alone
beside a silent telephone
or the dress lies ruined on the grass
or the girl walks off the overpass,

and all things flow out from that source
along their fatal watercourse.
However bad or overlong
such a film can do no wrong,

so when his native twang shows through
or when the boom dips into view
or when her speech starts to betray
its adaptation from the play,

I think to when we opened cold
on a starlit gutter, running gold
with the neon of a drugstore sign
and I'd read into its blazing line:

forget the ink, the milk, the blood –
all was washed clean with the flood
we rose up from the falling waters
the fallen rain's own sons and daughters

and none of this, none of this matters.

Peter Porter

No Heaven Cold Enough

Suddenly the worlds of death and substance seem to pause
in their mechanical obedience to the rules of time

And tension: we, the holders of Philosophy's new Bibles,
look away from everything we know corrodes, and speak

Pentecostally if cautiously of the Plan of Man, the engines
of his mind's consistency, the freedom from delay his towers

Know, forever rising from cartographies of hope!
But the ghost which Yeats would revel in will not be sent

Out naked on the roads for punishment – no element
may carry life's prefigured comical audacity

Beyond its blood-veiled site: nothing waiting on this moment
or this pen will freeze the spirit to a mind-free shape.

SHAKESPEARE'S DEFEAT

No one has ever been his equal
Yet quizzing him in doggerel
Is any Tribune's timid right:
All language is dispersed in light.

The Ordinary sunk in ordinariness
Say he is bald and hard to guess.
The Archons think to find a focus
Might tear its petals from the crocus.

Country Wisdom's top Townee,
His Coat of Arms Complicity –
The bubo of the world when squeezed
Is odium, yet some are pleased.

The Adam Smithy of our need
Commands both vile and pedigree'd.
So Mouldy, Feeble and Bullcalf
Get pricked: the audience gets to laugh.

His works are like Miss Emin's tent –
She sleeps with all, not just the bent,
But stencilled on the flapping walls
Legitimation calls and calls.

Music does it better, so
He has a journey shortly to go
But never come to that fine palace
Up a beanstalk from the phallus.

We writers want him as our Prince
The crazy public to convince
But would he even place a bet
On redemption via the Internet?

The dark house and detested wife:
After marriage, get a life!
Start out defeated – the glory is
Your Art shall seem victorious.

Christopher Reid

A Scattering

I expect you've seen the footage: elephants,
finding the bones of one of their own kind
dropped by the wayside, picked clean by scavengers
and the sun, then untidily left there,
    decide to do something about it.

But what, exactly? They can't, of course,
reassemble the old elephant magnificence;
they can't even make a tidier heap. But they can
hook up bones with their trunks and chuck them
    this way and that way. So they do.

And their scattering has an air
of deliberate ritual, ancient and necessary.
Their great size, too, makes them the very
embodiment of grief, while the play of their trunks
    lends sprezzatura.

Elephants puzzling out
the anagram of their own anatomy,
elephants at their abstracted lamentations –
may their spirit guide me as I place
    my own sad thoughts in new, hopeful arrangements.

AFTERLIFE

As if she couldn't bear not to be busy and useful
after her death, she willed her body to medical science.

Today, as a number of times before, I walked
past the institution that took her gift, and thought,

'That's where my dead wife lives. I hope they're treating her kindly.'

The dark brick, the depthless windows, gave nothing away,
but the place seemed preferable to either Heaven or Hell,

whose multitudes meekly receive whatever the design teams
and PR whizzes of religion have conjured up for them.

My wife is in there, somewhere, doing practical work:
her organs and tissues are educating young doctors

or helping researchers outwit the disease that outwitted her.
So it's a hallowed patch of London for me now.

But it's not a graveyard, to dawdle and remember and mope in,
and I had work to do, too, in a different part of town.

Hugo Williams

POEMS TO MY MOTHER

"You're the top, you're an ocean liner.
You're the top, you're Margaret Vyner."
- Cole Porter

1. THE CULL

You sit with your address book
open on your knee,
gently but firmly
crossing out the names
of old friends who have died.
'I wonder what happened
to Kay Morrow?' you ask.
'It doesn't matter,
I never liked her really.'
Your pen hovers briefly
over the head of the bridesmaid
we've heard so much about,
then slices her in two.

You have the look of a job well done
as stragglers are rounded up
for demolition.
'Dear old Denny Moon!
He taught me to ride.
He used to jump out from behind a tree
cracking a banksia whip.
That, or driving an old Lancia
between kerosene tins.'
You shake your head at him.
In spite of all the fun
you smile with quiet satisfaction
as you let him slip away.

2. New South Wales, 1920

A hundred miles ahead of the drought
and behind on the payments
you were on your way
to start a new life in New South Wales
when the car broke down
under a coolabar tree
and your father said it was The End.

He made you get down
and wait in the shade of the tree
while he went and stood on his own.
You thought you had arrived in New South Wales
and could start to explore,
till you looked behind the tree
and saw the bush stretching away.

He brought your luggage over
to where you were sitting
and started sprinkling petrol over the car.
You thought he was cooling it down
and giving it a clean,
before you set out once more
for your new life in New South Wales.

3. Only Child

Your front wheel runs ahead of you
through the yew tree tunnels.
The berries lie in your path,
like days for you to thread.
You jam your brakes
and fly ahead of your plans.
Your elbows are grazed.
Your handlebars are askew.
Someone has to straighten them for you.

4. Someone's Girlfriend

I'd met him before, of course, at somewhere like
Government House in Sydney, then again
in a nightclub in Le Touquet, doing my nut
trying to get him to light my cigarette.
I'd heard he was going to be in this
Freddie Lonsdale play on Broadway, *Half a Loaf*,
so I got my agent to fix me an interview
with the director, Gilbert Miller,
who threw me the part of someone's girlfriend.
When your father saw me sitting there
in the dining room of the *SS Washington*,
drinking my glass of milk, he thought he'd just
discovered me. He sent a note to my table
saying 'Champagne better than milk,
why don't you join me?'
                              I remember it was evening
when we arrived in New York Harbour.
Guy Middleton and Frank Lawton came down
to meet the boat in their dinner jackets
and took us back to a party. Your father and I
were staying at the Gotham, but it wasn't long
before we moved to the Devil, which was just as well,
I suppose, considering he was still married.

5. Café de Paris, 1940

I borrowed this totally embroidered
low-cut figure-hugging dress
for some charity do at the Café de Paris.
I was there to be decorative
and pose with a white pekinese,
while Lucienne Boyer sang 'Parlez-moi d'amour'.
Esmé Harmsworth won the tiara,
or someone gave it to her.

Oh, and I'll tell you who else was there,
Douglas Byng, 'The Cock of the North'.
He came on in this terrible kilt
with his usual monocle and twitch
and sang 'Flora Macdonald'.
Then there were The Yacht Club Boys:
'The huntsman said he'd found the scent.
We wondered what the huntsman meant.'

We all had to go up on stage afterwards
and Tony Kimmins, he was the organiser,
trod on my train, which immediately came off,
revealing the backs of my legs.
I let fly with a stream of invective,
which everyone heard apparently.
Tony always said he hadn't realised I was
Australian until that moment.

6. A Conjuring Trick

The undertaker slips me a folded envelope
in which he has caused to appear
her teeth and wedding ring.
His hand closes over mine.
His smile seems to require my approval
for his conjuring trick.

I feel inclined to applaud his skill
in so reducing flesh and bone
to this brief summary,
until I see his scuffed grey moccasins
and moth-eaten opera hat
with the folding mechanism showing through.

He takes me aside
and whispers that her ashes

will be waiting for me in Reception.
As we crunch back to the cars, we turn
and see smoke spiralling into the air,
while something difficult is imagined.

7. I.M. M.V.

You finally took the bait
You had cast some time before
You took the line in your mouth
You ran a mile or more

You hurled yourself in the air
You dived to the ocean floor
You came to the end of your breath
You wound yourself in to shore

Shortlisted Poems
The Felix Dennis Prize for Best First Collection

Siân Hughes

Mummy has to go now. Sorry we were late.
I brought you a flower. No, it's dead.

When you cut them, you see, they die.
The petals were white when I left.

I was sewing your name tags.
This is your name. I know it's no use to you now.

Home clothes are not allowed. It's the rules.
Your shawl is taped to your parcel.

Don't be afraid. You are not alone,
and no one has a bed with a window.

The man with the spade brings you in
from the rain. The one in black says words.

In a few weeks they'll come back
and let in more new friends.

The view changes each time. The sky,
believe me, is not always this cold.

When I was a little girl like you
I liked to peep through the banisters

and see who was calling so late.
My parents in their fancy clothes

might turn and say 'Who's out of bed?'
The visitors blew kisses. Sometimes

they saved me something special
that the grown-ups had to eat.

My darling, sleep well in your bed.
Don't come out on the landing where it's cold

because, you see, I won't come home
in my long dress and necklace

and blow you kisses up the stairs.
I won't carry you back to bed

to rub your blue feet better
or fetch blankets from the box.

No, you don't need a bottle, cuddle,
special rabbit, teddy, bit of cloth.

You don't even need to close your eyes.
They were born that way, sealed shut.

You are a hard lesson to learn,
soft though you are, and transparent.

There's a mark on your forehead –
the simple flaw that separates
the living from the dead.

It looks like I dropped you downstairs.
I didn't. I promise. It was like this:

somebody did some counting
and when they added you up

they found one part of you didn't match.
It's supposed to come out even.

They call it trisomy twenty-one.
It's not such a lucky number.

No, I know it doesn't begin to explain
your lack of Christmas presents

or the colour of your skin. I know
the best smiles in the world come out uneven.

Sleep Training

This is a lifeskill, and I will learn
to go back to sleep without crying.
It is normal to find myself alone
at night. It is normal to call out
and for no one to come. I will adjust.

Already I barely acknowledge the sound
of my screaming, night after night.
It is almost like silence to me, almost
like the night itself. I will learn
to close the door, turn aside, and sleep.

Emma Jones

Candles – why wave your hands about that way?
    Your wicks throw out inappropriate shadows.
    You can't be gothic before gothic *was*
        you know, and Mary Wollstonecraft
        hasn't given birth to Mary Shelley yet.

Not quite. There are two more minutes. The eigh-
    teenth century has a cough and Mary Senior
    is slack and all shifty in the bed with its
        half-expired shawls and its literary sweat
        where she's lain, she feels, for a thousand years

till, two minutes up, Mary Junior shows just her face,
    a wet homunculus, and Frankenstein's monster
    hides under the bed, and Mary Senior dies
        two-headed (death hasn't read
        'A Vindication on the Rights of Woman')

and Percy Bysshe Shelley, still a boy, dreams with the face
    of a drowned man of the Campo dei Fiori,
    where, just then, someone wakes up, and stands,
        and lights a candle to the Virgin Mary, whose
        'mystical rose' coughed the Word up like a pearl.

Sonnet

Here it is again, spring, 'the renewal'.
People have written about this before.
And the people who track the four seasons,
the hunters who know the weather has changed.

Still, rains happen; there are slow roots that make
progress; something has a hand in the earth
and turns it. Clouds unknot the wind. Bulbs blow.
Their threadbare minds gust outward, turn yellow

eyes to heaven. It answers with the sun.
And the sun is a bulb, a mutual bomb.
The daffodils crack. 'Oh heavens!' they fret,

'Where's your terminus?' The flowers are wan
travellers. They unpack their cases. All
they know, they are. Renewal, rest. Renewal.

Meirion Jordan

CRY WOLF

Once I was told that long ago
there were no poems, only wolves.
Poets would spend weeks
by the winter hearth, sharpening bone
until it grinned in the firelight,
splitting flints down to the last vowel.
Then as the night filled with snow
they would go out like ghosts through the woods
and return with great snarling pelts,
some of which can still be seen.
It is safer now. Nobody
loses an eye or a hand
to metaphor these days. And though
some people, in the high Carpathians
or among the Urals' snaggled vertebrae
claim to have seen the real thing,
most bring back dog skin, badly dyed.
Now we gaze hungrily
through the windows of museums
at the crooked smiles and glass eyes,
the weave of dust that was wolves:
in a few towns you can queue
down corridors of fishbowl glass
for your chance to shoot their relics.

Calculus

I have been wearing the rhythms of the sea
all day, the swing of it rising in my arms,
my fingers scathing the backwash
for the solidus of flat stones, raising them
firm as words in my fist and then
pitching their ellipses back,
their shadows meeting them as they kiss
the meniscus over and over with the lightness
of an eclipse. The wavefronts
hardly gulp as they go under but already
I have thrown another, skimming it
further, each one further over the sea,
over the universe's edge, their arcs
extending as they skip into the gaps between stars.
Stones you can't ignore. And here behind me
I might have a crowd, an idler dragging out
the dogend of the day. Probably none.
I will be here 'til the beachcombers are gone,
the massive sun washed up on the horizon.
The sunbathers depart. The swimmers.
Soon I will be alone. Tonight
I will be out late, then very late,
turning my pebbles at the spinning moon.

Lorraine Mariner

SUNTAN

The last time Jessica Elton had a suntan
she was eleven years old. Over the summer holidays
her mother would lock her out of the house
after her cornflakes and wouldn't let her back in
until her father got home. Jessica then spent
the next six weeks with red-headed Ian Morrison
playing ball girl to his Boris Becker, assistant
to his Doctor Who, victim to his Jaws
at the swimming pool. When she turned twelve
Jessica discovered the bean bags at the public library
and Victorian novels. For three days, Ian stood baffled
outside the window of the children's section,
a sudden orphan, turning a dangerous shade of pink.

INJURED

At school I always wanted to get injured.
To have crutches and a whole group of new friends
trailing me at playtime, or stitches, or a serious illness,
say diabetes (like my oldest friend Nicola's dad)
fussed over by the mother of a birthday party
with my own special plate of sugar-free finger food.
Like Katrina, who broke her arm one lunchtime
and was made to do PE that afternoon by her
unsympathetic teacher, who always had her favourites
and didn't believe her. When my forearm ached years later
it would have been a pleasure to remember the faces
of Mrs Hunt and her pets, as I came in the next day
with my father wanting a word and my plaster cast
like an exclamation mark, white against the blackboard.

J O Morgan

from SEE THIS BOY

See this boy – this Rocky.

At three years: the back door opened.
Out he goes. Prompted. Prodded. Pushed.
Squat body. Crew-cut. Short trousers. Green vest.
Little fists clenched into little pink rocks.

> *He'll be a hardy wee bugger this one.*

His father. Nailing the child's bedroom window open.
Four inch gap. Forever. No curtain.

The third of three children; the Benjamin.
Following the second sister by five years.
No more to come after.

> *He's been up and running*
> *for half his whole life.*

His mother. Allowing the wind to slam shut the door.

> *Let him play out where my legs*
> *are least likely to find him.*
> *And if he doesn't come back when called*

The father again:

> *then it'll be the webbing belt.*

his Victorian ideals coming fifty years too late.

And this boy – this Rocky – takes to it, quick.
An t-Eilean Sgitheanach. The Wingéd Isle. Isle of Skye. His.

And when they later call his name
over wind, over heath, over burn, over bog

he doesn't hear, and he doesn't come.

———————————

At home it's the Gaelic that rolls from his tongue.
Although he need not speak it very much.

The language of streams, of rock, of wood –
of nettles, as taught by their stings:
that handled right can make a three-fold cord
yet firm enough to catch a full-grown hare
and hold it fast – is much more to his liking.

The tongue of the classroom is English.

> *Read the words as you've been taught,*
> *or weren't you even listening.*

As in a dream the letters stay as letters.
They are glue. Have no perspective depth.
Their shapes mean nothing other than their shapes.
Have no relevance to sound, to throat. Un-word-like.

> *We know that you're not stupid.*
> *A stupid child can't hook a fish by hand.*
> *Your sisters aren't stupid.*

Suspicions are he might not be all there. Close.
Frustrated taunting blinds them to the link.

So when he shakes his head and does not speak
the teacher makes him wear a tall white hat
then stands him by the back wall of her class

– a remedy that's always worked before.

Beneath the narrow cone the boy
thinks hard on what he has or has not done.

His own solution: NOT TO GO TO SCHOOL.

His teaching to be gathered from the earth.
From scrub and thicket: *profit*, never dearth.

Meghan O'Rourke

DESCENT

I was born a bastard in an amphetamine spree,
    lit through with a mother's quickenings,

burrowing into her, afraid she would not have me,
    and she would not have me.

I dropped out down below the knees
    of a rickrack halterdress,

sheeted, tented knees, water breaking, linoleum peeling,
    and no one there to see but me,

I woke on the floor as if meant to
    put her back together, to try to hold on to her

like a crate to a river, as if I'd been shipped down
    to stand straight while in the misgiving

she said *I had a dream of thirty-six sticks*
    floating down a river and a dog who couldn't swim

and I could not swim, I slipped from her grip
    in a room where two orange cats stared

like tidy strangers at a world of larger strangeness,
    and I had no name, I was there at her breast

and I thought I could see her, the swag of her hair, the jaw,
    the fearing, but I barely saw, I went sliding down the river

from a house in which it was sweet to sleep,
     and the cool of the sheets

was never cool enough, and the imprint of the bedded bodies
     diving, at once, took the shape of two geese.

PALIMPSEST

So the days go by, and the singing at night continues.
The summer passes like horses.
Wisdom arrives on a piece of paper, blown
through wide glass windows:
"This page intentionally left blank."
I talk to my friends more than I used to.
I sleep less. This is the point of life:
you really care. The tendons slacken,
the fat honeycombs beneath the skin,
a fox paces in the town courtyard,
until, passing a mirror, on the phone,
laughing, you see yourself again
as you are, as you are not.
The snow creaks underfoot.
Touch me, I am still here,
like the humming bee, like the mayrope
wrapped around the tree.
The song was never mine to sing.
It lives beneath the skin.
It speaks in every bone.

Shortlisted Poems
The Forward Prize for Best Single Poem

Paul Farley

MOLES

Any walk into the hills
begins with the surprise of height
gained suddenly, over the shoulder
a view further than you thought you'd earned.

It was like this for Orpheus
looking back into the Underworld,
except this was happening in reverse
and it came towards the end of the climb.

Within sight of the blue of the sky,
with meadow scents and the song of birds
as the gradient slackened, he looked back to find
more emptiness than he thought earth held.

In this version of the myth
we leave him there, helpless and blind,
skimming for worms in the topsoil, cursed
with shovels that can't even hold a lyre.

Michael Longley

I have flown the Atlantic
To reach you in your chair.
Cuddling up, we talk about
Flowers, important things,
And hold hands to celebrate
Spring gentian's heavenly
(Strictly speaking) blue.
You grow anemones,
You say, wind's daughters.
I say the world should name
A flower after you, Stanley.
We read each other poems.
You who'll be a hundred soon
Take forever to sign
My copy of *Passing Through*.
What flower can I offer you
From Ireland? Bog asphodel
Is the colour of your shirt.
Grass of Parnassus? Mountain
Everlasting in New York?
Your zimmer-gavotte suggests
Madder with its goose-grassy
Tenacity, your age-spots
Winter-flowering mudwort.
But no, no. Let it be
Spring gentian, summer sky
At sunset, Athene's eyes,
Five petals, earthbound star.

Robin Robertson

At Roane Head

for John Burnside

You'd know her house by the drawn blinds –
by the cormorants pitched on the boundary wall,
the black crosses of their wings hung out to dry.
You'd tell it by the quicken and the pine that hid it
from the sea and from the brief light of the sun,
and by Aonghas the collie, lying at the door
where he died: a rack of bones like a sprung trap.

A fork of barnacle geese came over, with that slow
squeak of rusty saws. The bitter sea's complaining pull
and roll; a whicker of pigeons, lifting in the wood.

She'd had four sons, I knew that well enough,
and each one wrong. All born blind, they say,
slack-jawed and simple, web-footed,
rickety as sticks. Beautiful faces, I'm told,
though blank as air.
Someone saw them once, outside, hirpling
down to the shore, chittering like rats,
and said they were fine swimmers,
but I would have guessed at that.

Her husband left her: said
they couldn't be his, they were more
fish than human;
he said they were beglamoured,
and searched their skin for the showing marks.

For years she tended each difficult flame:
their tight, flickering bodies.
Each night she closed
the scales of their eyes to smoor the fire.

Until he came again,
that last time,
thick with drink, saying
he'd had enough of this,
all this witchery,
and made them stand
in a row by their beds,
twitching. Their hands
flapped; herring-eyes
rolled in their heads.
He went along the line
relaxing them
one after another
with a small knife.

They say she goes out every night to lay
blankets on the graves to keep them warm.
It would put the heart across you, all that grief.

There was an otter worrying in the leaves, a heron
loping slow over the water when I came
at scraich of day, back to her door.

She'd hung four stones in a necklace, wore
four rings on the hand that led me past the room
with four small candles burning
which she called 'the room of rain'.
Milky smoke poured up from the grate
like a waterfall in reverse
and she said my name,
and it was the only thing
and the last thing that she said.

She gave me a skylark's egg in a bed of frost;
gave me twists of my four sons' hair; gave me
her husband's head in a wooden box.
Then she gave me the sealskin, and I put it on.

Elizabeth Speller

This is the Pointe du Raz,
this place is Finistère,
the fall, the undertow, the earth's end where
my father's face is bones beneath the feathers of his blown back hair.
Tears in his mica eyes, spray on his skin
here on the Pointe du Raz the salted man leans in
to the force of wind and the rough, wet air.
Keep blowing east to landfall, wind
from sea to earth, from dark beyond
the razor's edge of Finistère;
keep him keep all my safety here.

George Szirtes

SONG

for Helen Suzman

Nothing happens until something does.
Everything remains just as it was
And all you hear is the distant buzz
Of nothing happening till something does.

A lot of small hands in a monstrous hall
can make the air vibrate
and even shake the wall;
a voice can break a plate
or glass, and one pale feather tip
the balance on a sinking ship.

It's the very same tune that has been sung
time and again by those
whose heavy fate has hung
on the weight that they oppose,
the weight by which are crushed
the broken voices of the hushed.

But give certain people a place to stand
a lever, a fulcrum, a weight,
however small the hand,
the object however great,
it is possible to prove
that even Earth may be made to move.

Nothing happens until something does,
and hands, however small,
fill the air so the buzz
of the broken fills the hall
as levers and fulcrums shift
and the heart like a weight begins to lift.

Nothing happens until something does.
Everything remains just as it was
And all you hear is the distant buzz
Of nothing happening. Then something does.

C K Williams

EITHER / OR

I.
My dream after the dream of more war: that for every brain
there exists a devil, a particular devil, hairy, scaly or slimy,
but compact enough to slot between lobes, and evil, implacably evil,
slicing at us from within, causing us to yield to the part
of the soul that argues itself to pieces, then reconstitutes as a club.

When I looked closely, though, at my world, it seemed to me devils
were insufficient to account for such terror, confusion, and hatred:
evil must be other than one by one, one at a time, it has to be general,
a palpable something like carbon-dioxide or ash that bleeds
over the hemispheres of the world as over the halves of the mind.

But could it really be that overarching? What of love, generosity,
pity? So I concluded there after all would have to be devils,
but mine, when I dug through the furrows to find him, seemed
                                                      listless,
mostly he spent his time honing his horns – little pronged things
like babies' erections, but sharp, sharp as the blade that guts the goat.

2.
Just as in the brain are devils, in the world are bees: bees are angels,
angels bees. Each person has his or her bee, and his or her angel,
not "guardian angel," not either one of those with "...drawn
                                              swords..."
who "...inflict chastisement..." but angels of presence, the presence
that flares in the conscience not as philosophers' fire, but bees'.

Bee-fire is love, angel-fire is too: both angels and bees evolve
from seen to unseen; both as you know from your childhood
have glittering wings but regarded too closely are dragons. Both,
like trappers, have fur on their legs, sticky with lickings of pollen:
for angels the sweetness is maddening; for bees it's part of the job.

Still, not in their wildest imaginings did the angel-bees reckon
to labor like mules, be trucked from meadow to mountain,
have their compasses fouled so they'd fall on their backs,
like old men, like me, dust to their diamond, dross to their ore,
but wondering as they do who in this cruel strew of matter will

save us.

Highly Commended Poems

2009

Lucy M Alford

OYSTERS

I

Kean's truck at the gate
　　brought them. Early June to my kitchen,
　　　　late.
Stopping off from the road this far
from town, he stood with the sack, the cold jar,
heavy in his hands, and rare.
How tall his frame in the waning pale,
　　how spare –

Got some oysters, he said. On sale.

II

At the counter on elbows,
　　first his fingers then mine
drew each splayed lobe
　　from the milky brine,
loaded the brittle thins
　　and trained the lolling skins
to the salted squares
　　of Saltines from another year

dug stale. Farther back, I
　　found Texas Pete's expired flask
crusting at the eye.
　　Besides the brown paper and glass,
preparation was spare:

clean plates and cold beer.

III

Strange organ, rudderless mollusk:

Whose tongue,
unglued at the nape,
whose folds?

The sea's split-lipped labia,
furled grey-pink and splayed
under thumb – unformed
in spill, then scooped,
assembled, and thrown
down the throat –

taste of iron
and glass,
old blood.

Unshelled invertebrate
in the throat's pull,
unsettled as the guest
colder than the ale.

Zeeba Ansari

MARRIAGE INTERVIEW

She says his mouth has lies in it as big as barns.
Grist for our mill, he grins, *and if you're wise
you'll come to my lap right now*

and have the grumble taken out of you.
There are pinks in her cheeks, her breasts
are a jug about to tip its cream,

but her purse isn't sure. Sugar and apples
make a good pie, but too little salt means
a pudding lacks spice, she says, and leads

to a life looking better behind than it does
in front. *I'll make perfect pastry to take you
from goodnight to good morning.*

What can you do with the planks of the heart?
*I'll make them into a nursing chair,
rock back and forth and fill its arms with babies.*

Can you make cheese? *I can make milk in the teat
come warm and blue.* Can you catch a horse?
I can whistle a mare at a town's distance

and she'll meet me with washed feet.
What do you pray for? *You, and you
telling me your fruits are three times*

ripe for eating. What about the calendar
of heaven? *I'll cover your holy days
with kisses.* And the common rules of love?

Better ask forgiveness than permission.

Ros Barber

MATERIAL

My mother was the hanky queen
when hanky meant a thing of cloth,
not paper tissues bought in packs
from late-night garages and shops,
but things for waving out of trains
and mopping the corners of your grief:
when hankies were material
she'd have one, always, up her sleeve.

Tucked in the wrist of every cardi,
a mum's embarrassment of lace
embroidered with a V for Viv,
spittled and scrubbed against my face.
And sometimes more than one fell out
as if she had a farm up there
where dried-up hankies fell in love
and mated, raising little squares.

She bought her own; I never did.
Hankies were presents from distant aunts
in boxed sets, with transparent covers
and script initials spelling *ponce*,
the naffest Christmas gift you'd get –
my brothers too, more often than not,
got male ones: serious, and grey,
and larger, like they had more snot.

It was hankies that closed department stores,
with headscarves, girdles, knitting wool
and trouser presses; homely props
you'd never find today in malls.
Hankies, which demanded irons,
and boiling to be purified

shuttered the doors of family stores
when those who used to buy them died.

And somehow, with the hanky's loss,
greengrocer George with his dodgy foot
delivering veg from a Comma van
is history, and the friendly butcher
who'd slip an extra sausage in,
the fishmonger whose marble slab
of haddock smoked the colour of yolks
and parcelled rows of local crab

lay opposite the dancing school
where Mrs White, with painted talons,
taught us *When You're Smiling* from
a stumbling, out of tune piano:
step-together, step-together, step-together,
point! The Annual Talent Show
when every mother, fencing tears,
would whip a hanky from their sleeve
and smudge the rouge from little dears.

Nostalgia only makes me old.
The innocence I want my brood
to cling on to like ten-bob notes
was killed in TV's lassitude.
And it was me that turned it on
to buy some time to write this poem
and eat bought biscuits I would bake
if I'd commit to being home.

There's never a hanky up my sleeve.
I raised neglected-looking kids,
the kind whose noses strangers clean.
What awkwardness in me forbids
me to keep tissues in my bag
when handy packs are 50p?

I miss material handkerchiefs,
their soft and hidden history.

But it isn't mine. I'll let it go.
My mother too, eventually,
who died not leaving handkerchiefs
but tissues and uncertainty:
and she would say, should I complain
of the scratchy and disposable,
that *this is your material*
to do with, daughter, what you will.

Peter Bennet

The Squirrel

'Not yet, perhaps not here, but in the end,
And somewhere like this.'
Philip Larkin

You talk to sunshine on the photograph
that blears our unremembered faces
and mirrors yours within a thin black frame.
Your flowers are very cheerful in their vases.
We did not wish you to be put in here,
or see your footprints as you drag your shins
beneath a floral dressing-gown
across the mop-slicks in the corridor.

Here's where you dream you tripped a snare
that closed forever on a whiff
of disinfectant and a pain that lingers.
You're like the squirrel on the chandelier,
we try to reach you, but our fingers
grasp only air, and up you go,
beyond our help, to where your name
comes vacantly from far below.

You planned to age like poetry:
lyric and elegy becoming one
in celebration of the verb *to be*.
To kiss you, we blot out the sun.
We did not wish you to be made of stuff
morphine can manage till your smile begins
to claim that dying is the same
as painless waking, and no damage done.

Paul Blake

Triboluminescence

Some diamonds start to glow when rubbed,
fluorescing blue or red. This can happen in cutting,
crimson running along the sharpest edge.

Band-Aid wrappers also exhibit this property:
the glassy paper sparking the electric blue
of a train slipping in the wet, although a plaster

will never do on wounds as deep as these.
Sugar, fatally white, gives off the light of dreams
ground or broken in the dark. Opened envelopes

prove to be full of storms, the violet flicker
of heat lightning along the horizon.
And the ceremonial spirit rattles of the Ute

hold crystals of quartz that glimmer through
translucent amber hide as they clash together.
They slowly gather dust in the glass drums

of museums, with the language that named them
Restless, unsated despite all we swallow,
our tribe takes no advice from spirits. And yet

we long for answers, so when skin is touched
roughly or gently and begins to shine,
we need to find new words in explanation.

John Burnside

Poppy Day

The butcher arrives with a love song
he learned from his father.

Out on the kill floor, veiled in a butterslick
circumflex of marrowfat and bone,
he rinses off the knife and goes to work,
his voice so sweet, the children come to hear

the beauty of it, slipped between a vein
and what the veal calf thought would last
forever.
                Barely a shudder rises through the hand
that holds the blade
                            and yet he guides it down
so gently, it falls open, like a flower.

And still the children come, to hear him sing,
his voice so soft, it's no more than a whisper.

Vahni Capildeo

FROM FIRST TO LAST HIS BOOKS, THAT STARTED THIN,
GREW LESS, AND I'D PUT MYSELF IN DEBT TO BUY ALL
FOUR OR FIVE OF THEM

Fame came to him at an age
when already long begun
was his way of moving off.
He wanted less of the words –
they were fewer, though not thought
pure; denser, pocked key-heads through
paper, as if resistless.
The most was, "I saw something".
Like ending a letter "Love",
he wrote, as if to people.
He was a generous man.

Ciaran Carson

In Ruins

but not
beyond salvation

as when after
the explosion

everything is
dormant that is

until the days
that are to come

fireweed
London Rocket

& convolvulus
erupting from

the nooks
& crannies

Anne Carson

WILDLY CONSTANT

Sky before dawn is blackish green.
Perhaps a sign.
I should learn more about signs.

Turning a corner to the harbour
the wind hits me
a punch in the face.

I always walk in the morning,
I don't know why anymore.
Life is short.

My shadow goes before me.
With its hood up
it looks like a foghorn.

Ice on the road.
Ice on the sidewalk.
Nowhere to step.

It's better to step
where the little black stones are.
Not so slippery.

I guess the little black stones
could be lava.
Or do I exoticise.

A man hurries past
with a small dog.
No one says Hello.

A pink schoolgirl passes.
Looks in my face.
No one says Hello.

Who would expect
to see a walking foghorn
out so early.

Wind pushes more.
I push back.
Almost home.

Why did I come here.
New wind every day.
Life is for pushing back.

Now it is dawn.
A gold eyelid opens
over the harbour.

People who live here
learn not to complain
about the wind.

I go inside and make tea.
Eat bran flakes.
Read three pages of Proust.

Proust is complaining
(it is 1914)
about the verb *savoir* as used by journalists.

He says they use it
not as a sign of the future
but as a sign of their desires –

sign of what they want the future to be.
What's wrong with that? I think.
I should learn more about signs.

The first thing I saw
the first morning I went out for a walk in Stykkishólmur
was a crow

as big as a chair.
What's that chair doing on top of that house? I thought
then it flapped away.

A crow that big is called a raven.
Corvus corax in Linnaeus's binomial system.
Each one makes a sound

like a whole townful of ravens
in the country I come from.
Three adjectives that recur

in the literature on ravens are
omnivorous.
Pernicious.

Monogamous.
I'm interested in monogamous.
I got married last May

and had my honeymoon in Stykkishólmur.
This year I returned to Stykkishólmur
to live with my husband

for three months in one small room.
This extreme monogamy
proved almost too much for us.

Rather than murder each other
we rented a second place
(Greta's house)

near the pool.
Now we are happily
duogamous.

There are ravens on the roof
of both places.
Perhaps they are the same ravens.

I can't tell.
If Roni Horn were here
she'd say ravens

are like water,
they are wildly constant.
They are a sign of Iceland.

I should learn more about signs.
I came to Stykkishólmur
to live in a library.

The library contains not books
but glaciers.
The glaciers are upright.

Silent.
As perfectly ordered as books would be.
But they are melted.

What would it be like
to live in a library
of melted books.

With sentences streaming over the floor
and all the punctuation
settled to the bottom as a residue.

It would be confusing.
Unforgivable.
A great adventure.

Roni Horn once told me
that one of the Antarctic explorers said
To be having an adventure

is a sign of incompetence.
When I am feeling
at my most incompetent

as I do in Stykkishólmur
many a dark morning
walking into the wind,

I try to conjure in mind
something that is the opposite of incompetence.
For example the egg.

This perfect form.
Perfect content.
Perfect food.

In your dreams
said a more recent explorer (Anna Freud)
you can have your eggs cooked as perfectly as you want

but you cannot eat them.
Sometimes at night
when I can't sleep

because of the wind
I go and stand
in the library of glaciers.

I stand in another world.
Not the past not the future.
Not paradise not reality not

a dream.
An *other* competence,
Wild and constant.

Who knows why it exists.
I stand amid glaciers.
Listen to the wind outside

falling towards me from the outer edges of night and space.
I have no theory
of why we are here

or what any of us is a sign of.
But a room of melted glaciers
rocking in the nightwind of Stykkishólmur

is a good place to ponder it.
Each glacier is lit from underneath
as memory is.

Proust says memory is of two kinds.
There is the daily struggle to recall
where we put our reading glasses

and there is a deeper gust of longing
that comes up from the bottom
of the heart

involuntarily.
At sudden times.
For surprise reasons.

Here is an excerpt from a letter Proust wrote
in 1913:
We think we no longer love our dead

but that is because we do not remember them:
suddenly
we catch sight of an old glove

and burst into tears.
Before leaving the library
I turn off the lights.

The glaciers go dark.
Then I return to Greta's house.
Wake up my husband.

Ask him to make us some eggs.

Billy Collins

AUBADE

If I lived across the street from myself
and I was sitting in the dark
on the edge of the bed
at five o'clock in the morning,

I might be wondering what the light
was doing on in my study at this hour,
yet here I am at my desk
in the study wondering the very same thing.

I know I did not have to rise so early
to cut open with a penknife
the bundles of papers at a newsstand
as the man across the street might be thinking.

Clearly, I am not a farmer or a milkman.
And I am not the man across the street
who sits in the dark because sleep
is his mother and he is one of her many orphans.

Maybe I am awake just to listen
to the faint, high-pitched ringing
of tungsten in the single lightbulb
which sounds like the rustling of trees.

Or is it my job simply to sit as still
as the glass of water on the night table
of the man across the street,
as still as the photograph of my wife in a frame?

But there's the first bird to deliver his call,
and there's the reason I am up –
to catch the three-note song of that bird
and now to wait with him for some reply.

Stewart Conn

CONUNDRUM

You'd think there would be a neat equation for how
when travelling by train the view from the window
and in the mirror opposite make clear we are hurtling
away from the past, and into our own future, at precisely

the same speed. Simple you say, just stating the obvious.
But it doesn't explain how images, as they recede, can
enlarge in the memory; tunnels ahead lengthen or shorten
consistent with levels of dread; surely as complex a concept

as you can come across. Even more, how an intrusive cell,
an invisible speck between sets of nerves, can have an impact
more catastrophic than a rock fissure or avalanche in a mountain
ravine; the tremor of an eyelid, cataclysmic as any fault-line.

David Constantine

FRIEZE

From blue a white Arcadia looks down
Over the bourg, the river and the silver mud
To a strip of foreground where the dead March grass
Is coming to life again in yellow coltsfoot

And we are wheeling my mother along the estuary,
She is in our midst, we wrap her the best we can
Against the bright snow wind, and flocks of voices
Have entered the space vacated by the sea

And following the tide, four generations of us,
Along the nearest edge of the warming earth
We reach a gate and passing through that gate,
She and her retinue, we are in among

A thicket of horses and she who is losing
All of the names we give to things and creatures
Loses the fear also, there seems no reason
Left anywhere in her to fear a strangeness

And the creatures flair this and are curious
To know a human frail as the moon in daylight
Seated small who lifts a hand (the light
Shines almost through) and not to fend them off

But bless and stroke and pat and have their nuzzling
And kisses. Queen she looks, ancient,
Or fearless girl among the hippocamps,
The crowding shoal of them with musing

Underwater eyes, who bow and lift their long
Heads over her and trail their salt and sticky
Manes and fringes, like the wrack and breakers
Far out on the returning sea, to feel.

If you could hear off the surface of these pictures
The crying of souls over the silver mudflats
You may pick up the conversation now
Engaged between my mother and the beasts,

Their snuffling and flubbering and snorting
And hers a soothing wondering little singsong,
An opened spring of present happiness
From elsewhere, way back, local, home. In me

That tone, the very note of her, revives
A child who offers up the gold of coltsfoot
To a whitehaired woman who inclines
Smiling to thank him from the background blue.

John F Deane

I too have gone down into my underworld
    seeking my father, as he went down into his;
we go on believing there is the possibility
    of discovering the rich knowledge that is held

like a life in amber and that we can return
    certain of what business we should be about. Here
is the very edge of dream, this the marsh, a green miasma
    hovering above; small birds, motionless, cling

to the reeds, like terror-stricken souls. You must cross
    in your journey, broad rivers spanned
by magnificent structures; you must cross, too,
    the laboured hills of Aquitaine and the neat

villages of Picardy. Great trucks go rushing by
    to somewhere that will not concern you; you pass
cherry trees by the roadside with their blood
    fruits, leave behind you

château, auberge, the diminished whisperings
    of wars; you will pass, too, fields of sunflowers,
those astonished and childish faces lifted
    in congregation. At a great distance the rough-cast

white of the highest mountains will appear at evening
    tipped with baby-pink; folk-art in medieval hill-top chapels
will draw out tears of innocence; in the baroque theatricals
    of later overwhelming churches, ghastly saints

will be sitting in their skeletal remains, grinning from glass caskets
    like dowdy stuffed birds; they shall remain for ever silent
and joyful on their couches. When you emerge, shaken, and carrying
    the ever-heavier burden of yourself, you may seek

solace in words, for the world burns to know what news
    the deepest darkness holds, but oh how you find
the words themselves pallid and languorous, so shy
    they lurk in hidden places like the most secretive

night animals. You will survive, you know, only as long
    as you hold to the narrow footpath, speaking your father's name
as if it served as talisman and wondering, when their time comes,
    will your children too go down into their underworld, seeking.

Jane Draycott

THE SQUARE

Across the square a woman is looking at me
from a window, the shadow of the room she's in
pressing her like a flower towards the light.

In her sleeveless linen dress she is beautiful,
a cool candle in the vast dark glass,
like my mother in a time before I knew her.

Between us, a river of tourists, faces lifted
to the great bronze horses stepping off
into some other air we cannot see.

Like a lover across a room I return her look
but she in her eyes is saying *It's too late now*
and it is: I might as well be invisible.

Even if I crossed the square and found
that room she's in, she would be gone for sure.
She isn't interested in me any more.

Joe Duggan

POET OF THE TROUBLES

Four years at university
to learn how to say
you're as frightened
or as disgusted or as dead
as some fella was
at Sparta or at Troy

Four years at university
and your words sound good
even though every time you symbolise
you lie and I can't blame you
I hide behind my four years
at University too

But my fingertips graze
on the rough of this brick
breath clasps, not sure
which way home is safest
is that car slowing down
or is it just me
can't find other words
for Belfast, for fear

Antony Dunn

LOVE POETRY

As if the bee wouldn't sooner hurl itself into a pub-garden pint
than knock itself out on the physics of how its wings shouldn't
                                        bear it up.

As if the bee doesn't know the better ways to employ a tongue
                                        that long
than droning on about aerodynamics of pollen streams and flight
                                        paths.

As if the bee would suffer a ceilidh-caller bawling the waggling
                                        steps
of its geometrics on paving of honey-light, the dusting of touch.

As if these bumbling words would do, butting at the walls of an
                                        upturned glass
when a lift of the lip would set the improbably beating creature off.

Simon Z East

i.
The weans –
Kayleigh's faither might have bin a
yellow-cab driver
        fae the Big Apple
two nights
the condom split. I dinnae mind
sometimes ah wis high
sometimes cleared a hundred an fifty
to go wi'oot.
Ma faither woulda bin proud.
            Ne'er look a gift horse...
Hamish looks like Nikolai. Nik took the strap tae me
like it were ma fault.
But no shortage of stiffs queuing to drink
ma canteens dry.
                    Special requests.
Fuck some cow six weeks shy of calving.
Hitched a' the way tae Linlithgow
twice a week, kinky bastard
one-time editor of the *S– – d*.
Fae the back,
                haun inside ma arse
ma fists grippin onto the shag
an tits lurching like weather balloons.

They're institutionalised three years now
like losin a lung or heart
never mind three digits.
                On the train back tae Glesga
ah spilt ma grief
onto the expenses form
                all blurry.

ii. 28th February, 2009
The scars –
                    like a diary or map all jumbled up,
like gouges in butter.
Photographed and catalogued.
An off-duty policeman cut ma neck open
and bit a tit.
                    Recognised him fae the streets.
The shite.
Hospital once extracted a wristwatch
an sewed up after a knife in ma anus.
Split ma knee
          while dangled fae a window
an a boyfriend's mates gagged an raped me
on huz sofa.

Nik often cut ma vulva
                    or stuck a revolver in ma ear.
Turned him on to hear ma sobbing
an stiffs like a scar he said.
                                   Not so many.
He guillotined a border terrier once
an pegged the head tae a washing line
to stop ma neighbours' complaining.
Doctor said
"Someone take a fuckin mace tae yer arse?"
but it was one of Hamish's trucks.
Also broke ma cheekbone
                    an cracked most o ma ribs.

iii.
Said his name was Alasdair
                    although ye can never be sure.
Wee round glasses an recited Rabbie Burns
                    like an angel.
Took me for a day-trip to the River Forth,

summer 2003.
Picnic with black muscat and kosher? ham,
murmurin water
                    an five stems of pink lilies.
Best day ah ever had.
Called me three days later from London,
said Sorry, you understand.
                              Course I did.

iv. November, 1991 (age: 14 years)

First time I did it to help a boy I was sweet on –
something ironic in that I reckon
(he owed a dealer or summat).
Lothian Road at midnight
                         knees trembling.
Massaged an old pervert's balls
and caught it clean in the throat,
worried he might smack me if I didnae.
            I got used tae the beatings after a while.
Ran back home along the railway cutting
crying
        and salt fumes in ma mouth.

v. 4:15am, 12th January 2009
Nikolai and Vassily three sheets tae the wind
mad wi it
crumpled cans like wasted penguins
                and powder remains oan the bread board.
After the inevitable —
Nik held ma neck
                    tae block the screaming
while his bawbag frien'
severed three fingers at the knuckles.
A long red ribbon of pain
            an the lights dissolving.

vi.
Entry in a primary school exercise book, dated 1984:

When I grow up I wanna be a model
or a pop star like Mad donna
or work in a lawndrete like me ma.

(P.S. I like animals to.

Carrie Etter

THE TRAPEZE ARTIST'S DEAR JOHN LETTER

I recede like a vanishing point on my ribboned trapeze
and trust hamstring and calf's steady marriage
when I hang from my knees.

Physics can name the force that pushes the bar away again.
I'd call it *Fortune's wheel* or *Tantalus's fruit*,
but then I'm the company tragedienne –

all good trapeze artists are. I no sooner arrive than leave.
I love you, I'm quitting you. I live my life between
the two meanings of cleave.

Katy Evans-Bush

To My Next Lover

All weekend I kept thinking about you:
as I cleaned the kitchen, changed my bed,
lay in the bath with a book, eyed up a waiter,
tried new perfume on, I thought about you –
bought new underwear – yes, especially then,
about you, looking into the mirror
in the changing room and again at home,
running my hands over lace, undoing clasps
(but only to put on the old ones and wash the windows).

I thought about your eyes across a crowd,
hooking into mine, unclasping mine,
as you come closer, breathing my perfume;
I thought about you while kneeling on the carpet
to reach a fork that was lying under the table;
I thought about you when Sharon on *Eastenders*
got into it with her adopted brother –
smashing all the vases where they fell –
I thought aboutcha then, lover, an' all.

Too long I've had no lover – just the last,
and that's no lover to speak of. I've been loveless,
clasped and virtuous, dreamless, skinless, tongueless:
but now I have you, Next, a leap to the future
tense: I'm thinking about your hips, your weight,
your possibilities, your previous lovers;
and even if it never happens, the kissing
of places beneath new lace, you'll still have been
my next lover, now. Thanks for the weekend.

Keri Finlayson

The Jazz Singer

Didn't we turn them out at night; the minstrels
The jesters, the painted fools?
Turn them out and lock the city gates?
Didn't we send the capering whores
And mothy bards off to sleep on matted straw
So they could show their hoaxes to the cows?
We knew that if we let them sleep within our walls
They'd make us stare bug eyed at their cavorting
And all would be a sleepless, endless loll.

But Pearl White flinches and we think:
        This is how it was.
Clara Bow flickers and we learn:
        This is how it will be.
Valentino tenses and we know:
        This is how it should have been.

Al Jolson steps up, recasts the net
Reels us in saying:

        *"Wait a minute, wait a minute
        You ain't heard nothing yet."*

Mark Ford

HOURGLASS

Early August, and the chestnuts
Are wilting – their splayed leaves
Tattered and blotched, their shadows, not understood, speaking
A forgotten tongue... tell, tell us where, their drugged sap
Must be sighing, tell us where our distress
Ends, where
Are the victories? Each pinched, each
Aching hour we grow sadder
And stranger: a rift
In the billowing cloud cover, this cage
Of rain, soft greyish
Swarms of nameless insects circling, alighting,
Settling, sustaining themselves,
A sandy, pockmarked
Wormcast, the deft sideways hop
And jab of a predatory
Speckled starling – are the shreds and fraying
Filaments
An irresolute wind
Is teasing
Apart, winnowing
And dispersing, strand
By strand by strand.

* * * *

"See," I grieved, "his mind
That so filtered
And sifted nature it made transparent her weirdest secrets, now lies
A broken prisoner of night. His neck
Droops, as if bowed with chains, and he sees nothing
But the cold, gaping ground." At this, fixing me
With her gimlet eyes, the strange woman answered: "But surely you

Are one of those who once lapped at my breast, and were raised
To tough-minded
Maturity on what I fed you? I armed you as well, yet you threw away
My weapons, not realizing
They would have kept you safe. Now
Do you recognize me?… You don't speak. Is it shame
Or stupefaction that keeps you silent? How I wish
It were shame!" Then, when she saw
My tongue and lips had utterly frozen, she approached
And laid a soothing hand
On my torso: "We must wait", she murmured, "for this fit
To pass. He'll know me soon enough, and then
Himself. For the moment let me wipe
Away some of the worries obscuring, like thick storm clouds,
His troubled sight." So speaking, she folded her dress
Into a pleat, and reached out, and with it dried my streaming eyes.

* * * *

Through
The valley ran a brook
In full spate. I descended, and passed a middle-aged woman kneeling
At its edge. She was washing potatoes. When I travel, I travel
Light, with just a few things in a knapsack, no sword
Hangs from my belt. And with my shaven head
I look like a priest, but I'm not, for I'm powdered
All over, from crown to foot, with the dust
Of the world… I reached home
Just as the leaves
Were turning, and my brothers and sisters
Gathered round, excitedly; but all I saw were wrinkles, dewlaps,
White eyebrows, and watery eyes. My older brother
Pressed into my hand a small purse, and said,
"Open it". Inside were a few strands of white hair
Preserved in a tiny glass case as relics
Of our mother. Nothing was the same, and it seemed

A miracle we were ourselves

Still alive. While I balanced
The frail, intertwined hairs in the palm
Of my hand, I kept imagining my tears
Dissolving them, their melting as an early autumn frost
Melts in morning rain.

Jacqueline Gabbitas

*

Grass looks out over the short field

I strop my edges blade against blade.
Skin.

I've known many blades, some
fired from minerals, cooled by rain.

Honed. They took me down
at the stomach. Knees.

From where I was left, I saw
man walking, legs sheathed in cloth

I strop my edges. Soon, they'll cut through
fabric. Tissue beneath.

*

Grass sings to her roots

red and yellow and pink and green –

He thinks, man, these are the colours
of air and water, of light and freeing –
but before this, they were ours:

our blades are green, our lowly stems
the red of poppies, pink of damask,
our rhizomes white as exemption.

And you, my loves, are palest yellow
like the long memory of sunlight
from a rainbow on a glacial floe.

*

Grass eavesdrops at a church window

If man would put his ear to this stained glass
he'd hear only my voice – the rush, the reed.

If he put his eye close, he'd see instead of *grass*
the body, veins, heads, broadcasting seed.

*

Grass makes way for Poppies

You know, you're swollen at the head
like some canker or gall.
And when your petals drop all
you leave are dry bells and headaches.

But can't you see how beautiful we are?
How deep red? How pure white?

*

Grass looks to the Mountains and listens to Moss

The sun's in my eyes.
You don't need your eyes to hear.

But the wind deafens me.
It's not everywhere – you know you've savannah
where right now the only wind is made by an animal
being brought down by another.

But I can't see the mountains from savannah.
*You know they are there. Listen! There are pools
and deserts you can hear from, glacial planes
that were once fields. What is legion if not grass?*

I don't know, Moss.
Can a plane remember that far back?

*

Grass sleeps and dreams of horses

The horses come back.
Black. Their mouths are bridled.
Their shins lacerated from my edges.

Field becomes desert.
I am under here, three, four fathoms
of sand. And the horses come back.

Desert becomes ice-desert.
I am seed and chaff in the melted core,
and man, face like a horse, looks down.

Ice-desert becomes town.
I am on the brow of a hill. A horse walks.
Her head hangs limply from her neck.

*

Grass understands Moon by her reflection in water

Many says I'm *wild rice*, but you know me,
my reeds and roots stretching out, under.

You've watched him harvest my seeds
in the early light, half yours, half sun's.

What does he know of light – he, who eats
it with no second thought – but its division
into names and properties? He says your light,
your beautiful halo, is cold, one of reflection.

For light, something must always burn,
even for yours, I wonder at your source.
I know it's the sun, but how do you earn
such love as hers? How did any of us?

Sam Gardiner

The Beauty of the Buttons

Wearing a coat of rain flaring to a skirt
of waterfalls she puddles the doorstep.
Behind the summoned silhouette
the room is dry and bright. Silver heads
rotate in turtle-necked pullovers
and a practised hysteric on a table
cranks up to a wolfhound's yowl on
'Irish bull romps home at ten to one!'
They snap their rings of teeth, jaws sprung
like traps, and whinny over how much
they save by having nothing more to lose.
Twenty minutes late, the back-lit shadow says,
you took your time getting here.
Did you assume that here would still be here
to be got to because without a here
there isn't a there? Yes, I thought so,
the shadow thinks, edged in light.
And either you were too slow to beat the rain
or the neighbourhood butchers,
who can't afford to miss a good war in colour,
planes rising into the sky like prayers
and bombs and missiles praising God mightily,
retracted their awnings as you approached.
Why, you might have been the Small Onion Lady
or the Beldam of Mercer Street come to let us know
about the Grand Closing Down Sale,
last few centuries, goodbye good buys, everything
must go, wet leaflets in your bleached hands.
Or perhaps you felt the need to share
your little secret that a stiff downpour
is as profound as a deep reflection,
and that one day you'll be glad of a day like this.
Step inside before you turn back to rain,

the light-eclipsing insoluble shadow says.
Our cardigans may be fully
though incorrectly buttoned but in any case
the beauty of buttons is that you don't hear
the screams or smell the burning flesh.
Distance fighters, brave only with the bow.
Or see the blood. But do come peacefully
out of the unknown and show us your samples
and explain how much whatever you're selling
would save us. The more visits we have
from civilisation the happier we are
it has nothing to do with us. She mops
her face with a tissue before disclosing that,
like a deep-strike precision guided missile,
she must be at the right address (16 Church St)
but in the wrong town, or we are.

Vona Groarke

Bodkin

A word from a dream, or several, spiked on it
like old receipts. Something akin to a clavicle's
bold airs; a measurement of antique land;
a keepsake brooch on a quilted silk bodice;
a firkin, filled to the brink with mead or milk;
a bobbin spinning like a back-road drunken bumpkin;
borrowed, half-baked prophecies in a foreign tongue;
a debunked uncle's thin bloodline; a Balkan
fairy-story, all broken bones poked inside out;
a bespoke book blacked in with Indian ink;
a bobolink in a buckeye or a bare-backed oak;
a barren spindle, choked ankle-high with lichen;
a fistful of ball-bearings dropped on a bodhrán.
Body skin. Kith and kin. Other buckled things.

Chris Hardy

DEFINITELY HUMAN

I expected him to be
pushed aside beneath a wall
out of the farmer's way
but he was abandoned
head down on a slope
half over on his side
looking stunned,
not my fault
I only had the one,
definitely human.

Before he was complete
he left his home on the mountain
to cross the ocean
and reach the city,
where he would be
adored, caressed,
become a man
full grown,
definitely human.

But he slipped
out of line
and cracked.
I can't explain how
I arrived here
from where I began
anymore than he can.
Imperfect, broken,
young,
definitely human.

No one could
heal his face
frozen in a blind
stone sleep.
Slumped, feet up
for the millennia to come,
thoughtless as a rock,
warm to touch in the sun,
definitely human.

Kevin Hart

THAT LIFE

There is a life I've barely lived at all
And, summer afternoons, I feel it brush
Against me, heading somewhere far away,

Up in the north perhaps where rain comes down
As if just thrown in vengeance for some wrong
No one remembers now, though people talk,

And in that life I stroll through open doors
And take the darkness offered every night
And am bewildered still by clocks and eyes.

It touches me, that breath, say once a year,
When rain hits thick and hard against the door,
When I have let my darkness have its way,

And then I almost know that other world,
And live in small hard words from years ago
And cannot be at peace in any life.

John Hartley Williams

CAFÉ DES ARTISTES

Mr Loneliness takes his usual seat
at the corner furthest from the door,
and moves the pepper pots aside
for a better view of the floor.

Waiting is what you do there
for a waiter who'll never come,
for a dish they've not invented yet,
for everyone, or anyone.

Waiting is what you do there
– attentively, or somnolently, with your fly
undone, or different coloured socks,
or a mustard-spattered tie.

The proprietor will soon emerge
to play his shrunken concertina
on which he captures seabird noises, or
the hoots of sinking steamers.

He'll accompany his honkings
with lyrics full of death and sex.
Fowl and flesh fly fast, or scamper nimblier
down the throats of guests.

And then he'll lift his matelot skirts
and do a hornpipe side by side
with Mr Loneliness, who feels again
the Angel of his Muse alive.

Using pepper pots as castanets,
spotless napkin tucked into his pocket,
Mr Loneliness dances as the ceiling fan
goes slowly round: *ockit ma-lockit ma-lockit*…

Who is this melancholy fellow?
This exo-skeleton? This rickety artiste
of tentacles and ink? They gawp, the customers,
to see such spectral leapings at the feast –

a hatstand sort of fellow, where the hats
of long-gone customers are tossed,
the scarves of women and the coats of bankers,
all the lost apparel of the lost…

Till silence follows music, except
the widdershins-revolving fan that ticks
its copper-bladed swastika and makes
a noise that someone really ought to fix.

Oli Hazzard

Moving In

You take me down to the crease in the hills
Where the farm's boundaries are smothered
By brambles and the dry stream-bed lies
Like a pelt – we follow it quietly, shoeless,
Listening to the waves at Calpe knead into
The beach, and reaching out my hand to
Touch your hair we are suddenly
Aware of the sensation that we are being
Overheard: yet all there is on this side
Of the valley is the fuzz of telephone
Wires overhead and darkness slowly
Encroaching behind the skin-pink clouds –
The orange trees, after all, seem to clutch themselves
Above the safflowers and alfalfas that
Spring from the ground like cocked eyebrows –
So, stepping onwards – stalking, by now –
Convinced that night is simply the folding over
Of fingers, leaned into a steeple – we hunt
For some burrow, some hood of earth
Where the sound of the sea is as unbroken
As it is within a coiled shell and build
A fire whose voice, like chicks-being-
Incessantly-hatched, will make our
Own seem all the more improbable. But
Now, as I sit alone, crumbling dry leaves
In my palm, it seems all I can dream of is
The onset of sleep. Really, I hardly notice
The rising heat of the circling brush fire that
Flays the whole sky of its stars.

Brian Henry

QUARANTINE

My father drowned in his bath
the year after I married a fitting death
for one so wedded to the earth
he hated water he rarely bathed
if one could die from stench
some nights at the river I thought
myself into his body slipped beneath
the water as he did lost my breath
as he did and forced myself not to fight
the lack of air as it bloomed inside me
as it did in him I like to think I held him
down when he struggled up for air
but I know he died asleep asleep
before his head went under he died
without pain in his stupor he died

Paul Henry

The Prayer Room

Your prayers could live in this room.
The clock would keep them in time.
It's late. There is lamplight
and moonlight, and two skylights.

Your eyes looked down on me
earlier. I could see the sea
when I tilted a pane and looked out.
Perhaps you heard me shout.
It is only three hundred miles.
I have heard men in gaols
call from cells to their wives
across busy roads, call to their loves.

If you came here now, and prayed
and taught me to pray…
If you came here once
to hear the clock, the silence,
I might close my eyes on myself
and simply forget myself
in your voice.

       Waves of prayers
break over me, my wasted years.
See how the tide takes me out
into darkness. But for this moonlight
I've disappeared. Who are we
but ghosts on the night's sea?

Your prayers could live inside me.
Say a prayer now, for company
and it may reach this lonely room.
I'll open a skylight in time
to let you in.

Sarah Hesketh

TULIPS

She has married the mouths of her tulips
with string. Five intermittent stitches loop
each gentle petal to the listing rim.
The light is all wrong for this time of year,
and the quiet fear that the blooms won't hold
assails her while she's drinking tea.
How difficult can it be for them
to hold their wealth until the wedding's here,
until her daughter's soft, untutored
hand, slips inside hers, confides her fear.
They'll slice each spilling thread together,
a mother's love, from an exploding cup.
In the garage a pile of wooden spools,
and a sewing box lid, that's tightly shut.

Selima Hill

CHARLIE'S GIRLFRIEND

When God made Charlie
He said 'Listen, Charlie,

soon I will be sending you
a girlfriend

and when you see her
you must *shriek at her*

and grab her by the hair
and then lean in

and peck her on the cheek
until she pouts

and starts to make
peculiar little *kissing-noises*

and this will mean *she loves you*!'
And I do!

I let him pinch the raisins
from my fruitcake

and hide them for him
in my ears and hair.

Ellen Hinsey

XVII
Correspondences

Aphorisms Regarding Impatience

1
Mythologies of the End
Each century believing itself poised as if on the edge of time.

2
The Meaning of Impatience
Restlessness in time. To imagine that which is not swiftly accomplished will never be fulfilled.

3
Displaced Envy
Unable to initiate creation, or manage civilization: the drive to engineer *decreation* with perfection.

4
Perplexing Instincts
The division of the spirit between advancement and abandon.

5
The Attraction of the Apocalypse
To control with absolute certainty one thing. And for it to be the last.

6
Fragile Vector
The intersection where civilization and perseverance meet.

7
The Effort of Civilization
Miraculous labor. Each day Sisyphus rolling his rock uphill
against the accidental nature of mankind.

8
Not a Solution
To draw into question Sisyphus's task.

9
Accepting Negative Inevitability
Intellectual sleepwalking. The ethical self abdicating
affirmation for the temptation of *renunciation*.

10
Deviant Logic
To reject contingencies of disaster. To glean *possibility* from
the crevices of *improbability*.

11
What is at Stake
The fragile geometry of the world held in hostage.

12
Not the End
A type of grace: waiting in impatience to see that, from now
until the far edge of always, *nothing happens*.

Clive James

THE AUSTRALIAN SUICIDE BOMBER'S HEAVENLY REWARD

Here I am, complaining as usual to Nicole Kidman
('Sometimes I think that to you I'm just a sex object')
While I watch Elle McPherson model her new range
Of minimalist lingerie.
Elle does it the way I told her,
Dancing slowly to theme music from *The Sirens*
As she puts the stuff on instead of taking it off.
Meanwhile, Naomi Watts is fluffing up the spare bed
For her re-run of that scene in *Mulholland Drive*
Where she gets it on with the brunette with the weird name.
In keeping with the requirements of ethnic origin
Naomi's partner here will be Portia de Rossi,
Who seems admirably hot for the whole idea.
On every level surface there are perfumed candles
And wind chimes tinkle on the moonlit terrace:
Kylie and Dannii are doing a great job.
(They fight a lot, but when I warn them they might miss
Their turn, they come to heel.)
Do you know, I was scared I might never make it?
All suited up in my dynamite new waistcoat,
I was listening to our spiritual leader –
Radiant his beard, elegant his uplifted finger –
As he enthrallingly outlined, not for the first time,
The blessings that awaited us upon the successful completion
Of our mission to obliterate the infidel.
He should never have said he was sorry
He wasn't going with us.
Somehow I found myself pushing the button early.
I remember his look of surprise
In the flash of light before everything went sideways,
And I thought I might have incurred Allah's displeasure.
But Allah, the Greatest, truly as great as they say –
Great in his glory, glorious in his greatness, you name it –

Was actually waiting for me at the front door of this place
With a few words of his own. 'You did the right thing.
Those were exactly the people to lower the boom on.
Did they really think that I, of all deities,
Was ever going to be saddled with all that shit?
I mean, *please*. Hello? Have we met?'
And so I was escorted by the Hockeyroos –
Who had kindly decided to dress for beach volleyball –
Into the antechamber where Cate Blanchett was waiting
In a white bias-cut evening gown and bare feet.
High maintenance, or what?
No wonder I was feeling a bit wrecked.
'You look,' she said, 'as if you could use a bath.'
She ran it for me, whisking the foam with her fingertips
While adding petals of hydrangeas and nasturtiums.
Down at her end, she opened a packet of Jaffas
And dropped them in, like blood into a cloud.

Christopher James

FAREWELL TO THE EARTH

We buried him with a potato in each hand
on New Year's Day when the ground was hard as luck,
wearing just cotton, his dancing shoes plus
a half bottle of pear cider to stave off the thirst.

In his breast pocket we left a taxi number
and a packet of sunflower seeds; at his feet was
the cricket bat he used to notch up a century
against the Fenstanton eleven

We dropped in his trowel and a shower of rosettes
then let the lid fall on his willow casket.
The sky was hard as enamel; there was
a callus of frost on the face of the fields.

Dust to dust; but this was no ordinary muck.
The burial plot was by his allotment, where
the water butt brimmed with algae and the shed door
swung and slammed as we shook back the soil.

During the service, my mother asked
the funeral director to leave; take away some hair
and the resemblance was to close; and yet
my father never looked so smart.

I kept expecting him to walk in, his brow
steaming with rain, soil under his fingernails
smelling of hot ashes and compost;
looking for fresh tea in the pot.

Anthony Joseph

A Widow's Lament in Guava Season
after William Carlos Williams
for Ursula and Mario Thomas in Malick

Sorrow is her dirt yard,
between the lime bush
and the tamarind,
where vervain creeps beneath
the latrine he left unfinished.
Thirty-five years
she lived with her husband.
Now the ripe mangoes just roll
downhill.
And the orange tree
sighs
as it sings in the sunlight,
its plaintive song of fruit.
And the sugar apple:
force ripe and some green.
But the suffer the love
in her heart blooms wild
like the jungle flowers near her bed.
And this morning as she waters them
she does not sing her morning song.
Today her son tells her,
'Mammy dem pumpkin
in de gully dat daddy did plant
like dey ready to cut'. He say,
'The pawpaw like it ripe too.'
And that night as she counts the fireflies
she wonders,
if the river keeps secrets,
will it hide her in its cool beneath?

Tamsin Kendrick

Peter Pan Versus Captain Hook

My friend vouched a theory that all men were either
Peter Pans or Captain Hooks. I don't know about you but

I know where I stand. Look what that bastard did to poor Wendy;
Tinkerbell too. I'll have no truck with flighty boys.

Give me instead the feel of steel on my thigh,
the screams of pirates trapped in the boo-boo box.

But most of all give me the whispery hair under the wig,
the gnarled hand, the hook trailing red lines down my abdomen.

He pulls my hair, holds his hook to *my* mouth, then, suddenly shy,
his mouth. No thimbles in sight. Finally, a real kiss.

Luke Kennard

Variations on Tears

I realise you never cry because the last of your tears have been anthologised as a *Collected* and you can't stand the idea of appendices. But what am I to make of the demonstrators playing cards with your daughters? Have they betrayed your estate? Go tell the children to gather their strength for the inevitable backlash.

I realise you never cry because each one of your tears contains a tiny stage on which a gorgeous, life-affirming comedy is always playing and it cheers you up the minute you begin. But what am I to make of the bare interior of your house? You're waiting for inspiration, right? Go tell the children to gather dust on the shelves of archive halls.

I realise you never cry because to do so would be to admit defeat to your harlequin tormentors – wringing their hands at the sides of their eyes and making bleating sounds – and you don't want to give them the satisfaction. But what am I to make of the *Make Your Own Make Your Own __ Kit*, the first instruction of which is 'Have a good idea for something'? Could I have not worked that out for myself? Go tell the children to gather followers for our new religion.

I realise you never cry because you are a total arsehole who cannot even muster enough compassion to feel sorry for *himself*. But what am I to make of your red, blotchy eyes when, as your pharmacist, I know for a fact you are not allergic to anything? Have you, after all, been crying? Go tell the children to gather my remains from the ditch and look out for the white bull who, I'm told, is still at large.

I realise you never cry because the last time you cried four separate murders were reported on the evening news, each one more grisly and inexplicable than the last, and you incorrectly assume there was a correlation. But what am I to make of this terrifying breakfast? Are you trying to get rid of me? Go tell the children to gather the farmers from their taverns to gather the new crop of thorns.

I realise you never cry because when you do, you are beset by birds with long tails and brightly coloured plumage and sharp, hook-like beaks who are uncontrollably drawn towards salt. But what am I to make of your statement, 'The world is not built on metaphors'? What exactly do you think the statement 'The world is not built on metaphors' is? Go tell the children to gather in the clearing and await further instruction.

Mimi Khalvati

AFTERWORD

for Archie

Not in my heart do I carry you
with me everywhere
since your death, but in my mind

have you accompany me –
pedestrian and passenger,
side by side on the top deck

or standing while I sit
when there's only a seat
for one of us on trains.

Not in my heart but in my mind
beside me, talking, while I
gaze out through a mist of green

as I have always sat with your absence.
Even the rain is green in London,
so much green in May.

*

This old lady with a black mark
on the back of her right hand –
like the outline of a tree in winter –

and the tenderness I feel for her
and she reciprocates, is nothing
like the women in my family

but is connected to me nevertheless.

We sit side by side on the plane
with a spare and empty seat between us.

This allows us to turn our heads and smile
without discomfort, at a natural distance,
or to watch each other surreptitiously

but with grace. I like that she looks at me.
The accompaniment and the separateness.
The mutual looking-after.

*

At the depth of my shins and calves,
a pale green filter, deepening
to the height of the pelvis, creates

a bridge to the deepening blue
of L'Outro bay, at first aquamarine,
then turquoise, then pewter blue,

then way out there where the hills
become like Chinese hills, hardly real,
the rulered royal blue of the horizon.

The green filter creates an aquarium
for stones, the large ones green as if
a layer of algae were swaying over them.

There are zigzag lightning lights in the water
and then, there where the cold will hit
my belly and breasts, the lightnings disappear.

*

Of your body what is left
but ash and a single hair?

A perfect ring, one coiled spring

of microscopic wire.
Archie, you are gone now
Gone, gone, gone. Gone utterly,

irrevocably, yes, you are.
Look how solid our buildings are,
how material the sky.

Paris is where you left it,
so am I.
I, small as a single hair,

the infinite divisible.
You the indivisible nowhere,
whole, entire.

*

Mid-afternoon when snorkellers,
knowing the sea has warmed sufficiently
for their old age, take to the waves,

so the waves too, for those who lie
listening with their eyes closed,
come like dolphins out to play –

their swishes and flurries creating
fish-shaped sounds to play across
their ears. Beside mine I place a shell,

a glint of mother of pearl on its whorl,
and think of that one last stray black curl
clinging to a tile back home for weeks,

months maybe, after your death.

The last bath I took, cleaning
the bath beforehand, washed it away.

*

There was a wall or kind of cupboard
and, caught between the louvred layers,
the elbow of a shirt I recognised

in the language of dream-recognitions
as my son's and I leapt on it as I would
a drowning child and, grasping some corner

of the shirt or sleeve, dragged it out
in one great slash from between the slats.
Last night a small boy slipped perilously near

the edge of the quay and his young mother
leapt from her chair to yell at him, pointing
at the dark night water, and I wondered

at anger and the fearsome tenderness
it springs from, the fear and helplessness
despite all our warnings and harangues.

*

Was it twice or three times
I woke from a nightmare?
Each nightmare twinned

to the one before, one
brother to the other.
Nothing is yet forgiven.

A sickness rises in me.
I will take it with me

on the long drive home

for I have nothing else to take –
no ring box, no sarong.
When I think of the word 'sickness'

childhood calls to be born again,
this time in the open air
with an open mouth.

*

As long I listen to birdsong,
I distinguish neither vowel nor consonant
and therefore can't describe it in words

though the rhythm does persist
like the rhythm of persistence itself.
And so you, being dead, are like birdsong

and the rhythm that persists is the afterword,
he's dead, he's dead, he's dead.
On one side of me at the beach today

were Italians, on the other, French.
And I revised my opinion of the French,
both the people and the language, finding them

charming, the fat women and the thin men.
(Only because you, who loved the French,
are dead.) Death has altered me too late.

*

There is a step up to the shower-closet –
the showerhead is blocked and I wash,
sluice myself half-squatting under the tap.

Through the shutters I see the back
of the chair on the balcony spread
like a fan. There is a ceiling fan.

My blanket is very soft at night, even
against my face. In the fridge are
half a melon, seeded, some apricots,

the last of a small pot of honey
and a knife. Wind bangs the door
at night even though it is locked.

I light a last cigarette. The nights
are black. Everything in my room
is white, including my pencil.

*

I am surrounded by the wild furniture
of Crete – boulders, light tan and grey,
cushions of sage, trees, low and branched,

forming a pool of shadow beside the church
against a choppy turquoise sea. Yet
I am drawn to the long bare stone table,

speckled where the whitewash has eroded,
a bench for the solitary and arthritic.
A poem should be a makeshift thing,

Bishop said and the spirit too needs
furniture to invite it in – otherwise
where would it be, lost on a headland
of heat and wind, nothing in its hands
to carry home, no home but a windy church
with a banging door, a music of wind and tin?

*

Imagine a corpse laid out on a hill.
Imagine a hillside with a goat
grazing halfway up it; the bell;

the wind; the difficulty, when a wind
blows really hard, of seeing.
But the sound rises; at one point,

almost sounds like singing.
There'd be birds circling, surely.
Here there are no birds – the odd seagull,

tilting in and out of visibility.
There'd be wolves, hyenas, jackals.
A quiet, concentrated tearing.

And a loping away to their young,
a red around the mouth like her sheep,
Louie was telling us, who love beet.

*

Yiorgos, you haven't fixed my shower yet
but every morning you glide to my table soundlessly
to bring me coffee with a deference I don't deserve.

If I thank you in Greek, you smile. After a year
you have cut your beard. Now you bring us brandy and cakes,
wheat, nuts and honey, for it's the one year anniversary

of your brother's death. Your mother, old now and heavy,
helped me carry my case up the steps. It was heavy
with paper and books and too many clothes to wear.

I was here last year as you remembered, clasping
my hand in yours, warmly in greeting. During the year,
now and then I thought of you sitting in your chair,

the long sea-gaze in your eyes. Man of few words,
here are a few for you: *efkaristo, kalimera, kalispera,*
and the silence that lies between them of a long sad year.

Katharine Kilalea

You Were a Bird

You were a bird before we met. I know that
because over your skew front teeth
your mouth makes a pointy beak.

I saw you first in Dickens' London,
an evening of frosted windows
and hot steaming steak.

That night we were drinking,
the chimneys were smoking,
and my lips swelled up

like bread baking in the oven.
I met London in your face,
I smelt wine on your breath

and the shape of your mouth
left me feeling slightly lyrical.
We drank a lot that night

we drank so much
you would have seen it from heaven.
With you there, sitting there in my kitchen,

the cooking pots start to sing.
Now the letterbox is a bird
and the telephone is made of birds when it rings.

John Kinsella

LUDLOW TUART FOREST RE-ENACTMENTS

That sing-song bulldozer,
canals along estuarial breathing-lines,

Géographe Bay straightened to a queue
of alexandrines:

        this exploration, these reeds
throwing shadows that never broaden,
less than remnants.

        Ibises cluster low
in low-water trees, flood control
reflex. *Living space.*

    Inward. Far enough
for the sound of the sea

to be a whisper; wetlands keelhauled
of reeds and paperbarks,

effigies of water.

      A cat prowls
further away from the house and shakes its bell
until the toll is forgotten.

        In there, over limestone
and sand, tuart forest gathers open space,
fire-rings vacuums for silhouettes
to fold.

    High and wide, rare and confined,
to move between tall tuarts at a leisurely pace. Edged

by Wonnerup Farm

where Edward laboured,
Anne bore children, away from the grand English house,
made a language out of Gaelic

that the English might understand. A place
to branch out from.

                              Sea-traffic, news and income:
the whalers: bones and oil exchanged for butter. Flocculation
and coalescence. Partial
oleochemistry.
                    The glaze of family portraits
not yet taken. Viscosity as measure of fealty – molecular structure
of chatter then silence.

Beneath, mineral sands. Ilmenite,
leucoxene, zircon. *Waiting*.

Makers of pasture-lands.
Police lines. Agencies.
Cows in the forest. Incorporation.
Heart-poison
stripped out.

                    There is no allegory,
no mysticism stirring
the leaves,

compensating.

                    Pray, heart-poison stripped out
at the beginning of the new beginning, pre
the post-Lapsarian tension
                              across hyphens,
enjambments

surveyed as settler families,
one of which, progeny of –

if not them, whom
can I criticise?

               Bystanders
to the main game.
Bussell clan

called out from family gathering,

summoned from praying,
fleet-footed on their horses
through the avenues
of wide trees: massacre hymns:

women, children, warriors. Scion
of Wonnerup Farm, Layman, pulled Gaywal's beard,
euphemised women.

                  Caretakers of The House
tell the tale, prosaic
in the telling. A disclaimer, never
caveats. Local
history married into, tended.

Like a pair of inked sheets of the massacre day
ripped from the Bussell diarist's
journal. Pepys. A day missed,
a day in day out, day excised,
that surcharge of evidence.

            Finely crafted binding,
presumed death by drowning
of the Frenchman, Vasse,

old words caught like Chaucer's English, back into play: Ludlow
and Vasse,
Englishman, Frenchman. Both named as river names
renamed.

DNA: fantasy: Dragon's Blood tree
by the old house Edward served, Irishman in thrall of, forest's edge.

awaiting the stalking egrets,
reinstatement of avocets

as a roadname: his own farm, own
secrecy.

And sand, so
much sand beneath the tuart trees. Some forest remains,
sand-miners blame
the name-game. Re-
enactment.

August Kleinzahler

Shoot the Freak

Shoot the freak Cold wind, boardwalk nearly empty *You know you*
                                                    wanna
A cluster of hip-hop Lubavitch punks, shirt tails out, talking tough
                                              You shoot him
he don't shoot back Keeper-flatties thrashing in buckets, out there on
                                                        the pier
Shoot the freakin' freak A regular family of man out there, fishing
                                                      for fluke
and blues in that wind *How you gonna build memories* Everything
                                              shut down
or gone *Let the lady have a try* Sponge Bob, Spookerama, Luna Park
Shoot 'im in the head the Mighty Atom, Thunderbolt, Wonder Wheel
He likes it when you shoot 'im in the face Surf House, Astroland,
                                                  Shutzkin's
knishes, *A real live human target* 'Hungry for Fun', fried clams
Everybody's gonna 'Bump yo' ass, bump bump bump yo' ass'
You know you wanna You know you wanna You know you wanna
And that's when we saw him, *him*, 120 million records sold
                                              worldwide
walking across the sand 'It's him, it's him' Like a god, with that hair
What does he do to keep it like that Looking good still, tall, slim,
                                              creased slacks
handmade Italian boots, a black goddess on his arm, like an older
                                        version of that chick
on Miles's *Sorcerer* album, wow The camera crew running all
                                      around them, frantic
He's waving his arm towards the ocean, telling her how it used to be
how it used to be when he was growing up close by, in Brighton
                                                    Beach
OhmyGodOhmyGod *Sweet Caroline, HollyHoly, You Don't Bring Me*
                                                    Flowers
the duet with you know who, the two of them in the choir together at
                                                  Lincoln High

the 1992 Christmas special, the White House concert, the time
he met Lady Di
('a great person, just a fabulous person, a real human being')
I mean how good is this, really, I mean really, seriously, how
good is this

David Knowles

So What Does it *Feel* Like?

There is this smooth ridge
on the front face of the throttles
like the big sinew on the back
of an old man's hand.
My fingers rest there.

There is the smell of hardly anything
mixed with hot wiring
and the silent hum of avionics
deep in the loft of the fuselage.
Over all a watercolour wash of AVTUR.

There is a noise comes into our silence
close to the place we are going.
The sound of *them and us* –
men fighting –
an intrusion of lock-on and jamming
a rag-bag of coordinates and talk-ons
heavy static, numbing interference.

There is a chink in the curtains
sometimes a flicker in the breeze
where doubt gets into a night cockpit
while my back is turned.

There is the familiar surprise
as I wait four long, drawn-out milliseconds
thumb hard down on the pickle button
held to account
    for not following the checklist
    for the failure of the mission
    for the wrong side's casualties
    the humiliation…

ended by the *knock-knock* of release.
There is a trip home, racks empty.
A hop, skip and a jump in an old jet
suddenly a young girl dancing
foot-light around finals.

Nothing can touch us now.

Derek Mahon

A COUNTRY ROAD

Above rising crops
the sun peeps like an eclipse
in a snow of hawthorn, and a breeze sings
its simple pleasure in the nature of things,
a tinkling ditch and a long field
where tractors growled.

Second by second
cloud swirls on the globe as though
political; lilacs listen to the wind,
watching birds circle in the yellow glow
of a spring day, in a sea stench
of kelp and trench.

Are we going to laugh
on the road as if the whole
show was set out for our grand synthesis?
Abandoned trailers sunk in leaves and turf,
slow erosion, waves on the boil...
We belong to this –

not as discrete
observing presences but as born
participants in the action, sharing of course
'the seminal substance of the universe'
with hedgerow, flower and thorn,
rook, rabbit and rat.

These longer days
bursting with sunlit fruit
and some vague confidence inspire besides
skittish bacteria, fungi, viruses, gastropods
squirming in earth and dirt.

Dark energies,
resisting gravity,
fling farther the red-shifting gas
but the lone bittern and the red grouse,
crying 'Go back!', have got the measure of it.
Animal, vegetable, mineral watch
as we walk their patch;

and a bath in the woods,
its brown depths where once
a bubbling foam of soap and juniper.
Now tar-water of Cloyne, cow faces, clouds,
ice of the winter months
and nobody there.

Nobody there
for days and nights but our own
curious thoughts in a storm or before dawn.
Bird, beast and flower, whatever your names are,
like the wind blowing through
we belong here too.

Jill McDonough

AUGUST 23, 1927: BARTOLOMEO VANZETTI
Charlestown, Massachusetts

He finally saw the *nighty, starry sky*
with guards escorting him from cell to death
house. Seven years, a judge who'd ask with pride
Did you see what I did to those anarchist bastards? Yet
he knew, without them, he would have lived and died
unmarked, unknown, a failure. With *some sins,*
but never crime. I've never committed crime
at all, at all.

       When Socrates' jailer came in
with the hemlock, he wept for Socrates, *the finest,*
best-tempered man of any in that place.

Vanzetti thanked his jailers for their kindness,
their help. They tightened straps and covered his face.
His warden wept when Vanzetti murmured he
would forgive *some people for what they are doing to me.*

Roger McGough

The Wrong Beds

Life is a hospital ward, and the beds we are put in
are the ones we don't want to be in.
We'd get better sooner if put over there by the window.
Or by the radiator, one could suffer easier there.

At night we dream of faraway places:
The Cote d'Azure, all perfume and light. Or nearer home
a cottage in the Cotswolds, a studio overlooking the sea.
The soul could be happier anywhere than where it happens to be.

Anywhere but here. We take our medicine daily,
nod politely, and grumble occasionally.
But it is out of our hands. Always the wrong place.
We didn't make our beds, but we lie in them.

Clive McWilliam

HOLDING ON

My tiny aunt was always afraid
she might be blown away. She fluttered about
in the draft of her house chasing snails
that slid under the door. Each night she climbed
a steepening stair to lie beneath the stars'
straining light, hidden in sodium glare.

Her four room cave in the shade of passing
buses, where daylight goes
to snooze, with two knotted dollies
standing guard in a chair
and a wardrobe of tiny shoes.

You must have left the door ajar
the night the snails brought you the light
of stars on their backs, for the wind got in
and swept your house and blew you clean away.

Deborah Moffatt

Along the Coast

All along the coast the young men lie in lonely rooms
Listening for the welcoming sighs of women lying alone
Behind doors left half-closed along darkened landings
On wet dreary nights in the long hours between the last drink
And the start of another day, a woman's sigh inviting the young men
To roam from room to room, from bed to bed, from lips to breast
To thighs, to the wine-drenched oblivion of passionless sex
That helps to pass the lonely night somewhere along the coast.

All along the coast the young men die a little every day,
Their lives slipping away in the hours spent tending bars
Or grooming greens, time spent waiting, watching, dreaming
Of possibilities that might arise, or rueing the chances missed,
Or listening to tales of other men's successes, tales retold,
Later, as their own, to bored women in lonely rooms
Who know better than to hope for anything more than this,
A night of passion in a dreary room somewhere along the coast.

All along the coast young boys with their fathers' faces
Dream of becoming the men their fathers might have been
As their lonely mothers take other men to their beds
On wet dreary nights in the long hours between the last drink
And the start of another day, while young men growing older
Sleep alone in rented rooms, their youth spent, their time gone,
Every dream abandoned, every penny wasted, every chance
Missed, young lives squandered and lost, all along the coast.

Sinéad Morrissey

History

Dear Heart, I dreamed a territory so seeming rich
and decorous, I woke with all its workings on my tongue.
Napoleon vanquished Europe. But when he died
(of natural causes) on the Palace-Garden Isle, *Isola Bella*,
built to resemble the rigging of ships, the map changed colour
from the Bay of Biscay to the Carpathian Peaks as bloodlessly
as the delicate octopus its rippling skin. The world shrugged off
his atheistic scarlet and dipped itself in yellow, the yellow of egg-
yolk and daylight's origin, and a Golden Age let down its iron bridge
and set us travelling. Everywhere was the same: commerce
was encouraged (though not excessively); order and cleanliness
governed and dignified both public and private realms; music
and poetry could be heard in all quarters. In Spain itself, the centre
of the empire, all were as one: Language, Religion, the Crafts of State,
and the people flourished and were happy, the sap in the veins
of a Body Politick in rigorous health. Women, ever the lynchpin,
of households and families, of the men who bear the imperial message
like a lamp into the dark, wore their mantle lightly, were softly-
spoken, modestly attired, and though at liberty to work and roam
abroad, turned all their passion inwards to their sons and homes...

                                                              Dear Heart,
travelling through Switzerland in a previous summer, we stopped
in Berne and witnessed the *Zytglogge*: a medieval tower of time.
Beneath its east main face is an intricate astronomical and astrological
device, wherein, in one small radius, are displayed:
all twenty-four hours, the hours of brightness, the days
of the week, our position in the zodiac, the date, the month, the progress
of the moon and the degree of elevation of the sun on the horizon.
It was raining that straightforward, European rain we seldom see
at home and a small crowd murmured to their umbrellas
as Caspar Brunner's parade of bears, Chronos with his hourglass,
and a grinning jester in cap and bells rattled out of the darkness

four minutes to the hour. And my dream was like this –
as these eight signposts to our mortal existences
clicked and chimed together, so the interlocking arms
of God and Man and Government danced flawlessly there.
What measure of exactness could keep my golden territory
intact and accurate to the second? That same year, but later,
a woman read my fortune in a brace of cards. One showed a cup,
for love, and another a blinded girl, and another a hill of wheels
and gibbets, stood stark against the sky as the Saviour's Cross.

Stanley Moss

AUTUMN

For Stanley Kunitz

In a dream after he died
I received picture postcards
from him every day for two weeks
in a single night – the picture:
blazing maples and walnut trees,
New England in full foliage.
I wept that he should write
to me and my wife in a handwriting not his
in blue ink so often.
Since I do not remember the text,
I suppose the message was:
"Every autumn you know where to find me."

Andrew Motion

FROM THE JOURNAL OF A DISAPPOINTED MAN

I discovered these men driving a new pile
into the pier. There was all the paraphernalia
of chains, pulleys, cranes, ropes and, as I said,
a wooden pile, a massive affair, swinging

over the water on a long wire hawser.
Everything else was in the massive style
as well, even the men; very powerful men;
very ruminative and silent men ignoring me.

Speech was not something to interest them,
and if they talked at all it was like this –
'Let go', or 'Hold tight': all monosyllables.
Nevertheless, by paying close attention

to the obscure movements of one working
on a ladder by the water's edge, I could tell
that for all their strength and experience
these men were up against a great difficulty.

I cannot say what. Everyone of the monsters
was silent on the subject – baffled I thought
at first, but then I realised indifferent
and tired, so tired of the whole business.

The man nearest to me, still saying nothing
but crossing his strong arms over his chest,
showed me that for all he cared the pile
could go on swinging until the crack of Doom.

I should say I watched them at least an hour
and, to do the men justice, their slow efforts

to overcome the secret problem did continue –
then gradually slackened and finally ceased.

One massive man after another abandoned
his position and leaned on the iron rail
to gaze down like a mystic into the water.
No one spoke; no one said what they saw;

though one fellow did spit, and with round eyes
followed the trajectory of his brown bolus
(he had been chewing tobacco)
on its slow descent into the same depths.

The foreman, and the most original thinker,
smoked a cigarette to relieve the tension.
Afterwards, and with a heavy kind of majesty,
he turned on his heel and walked away.

With this eclipse of interest, the incident
was suddenly closed. First in ones and twos,
then altogether, the men followed. That left
the pile still in mid-air, and me of course.

Christopher North

TAINO

(Federico Borrell Garcia, "Taino" from Benilloba, near Alcoy was photographed at the moment of his death in a skirmish at Cerro Muriano near Cordoba by Robert Capa on the 5th September 1936. The photograph 'Falling Militiaman' became one of the best known images of the Spanish Civil War.)

He knew the ridge above Pico de Pedrera.
Each morning he saw the sun catch its flank –
that instant, just as the roosters started up.

Then came the rattling of blinds,
Inmaculada flicking water to settle the dust
and a sudden cracked note from the church tower.

Coffee, tostada with oil,
his older brother sprawled in the doorway
fiddling with a shotgun

and grunting at him when he stepped past
to catch the truck to the mill.
That's how it had been day following day,

so he was surprised
at the force of his brother's embrace
and the embarrassed, gruff kiss

when he stood at attention before him
polished and smiling
before leaving for Cordoba and the front.

His mother's face grey, her smile of stone –
he'd not seen that before either.
Cards from the poker game with his younger brothers

were still splayed on the table –
there was a centimeter left in the wine bottle.
That was 1936 in Benilloba. It's an Arab name.

Sean O'Brien

The Landing-Stage

For Derek Mahon

Like one surprised yet tolerant,
You walk out of the darkness now
To speak to those you cannot see
Or quite believe in, though the place
Is stowed to bursting with the crowd
Who are, like foreign policy,
Especially concerned with you.

Now that you take the floor at last
We see it is a landing-stage, new-built
For the Odyssean returnee –
Port in a storm or final anchorage
No one can tell but you perhaps
Who even as you speak to us
Take care to keep your counsel still.

In our unheroic age
You have sustained a northern clarity
Enriched with the harmonics of the south,
And learned to voice whatever is the case
For wisdom's and its own sweet sake
As music, intimate and vast.
You let the grave itself unstop its mouth.

You tell the language that your love
Endures, whatever you have undergone
Of shipwreck or dry-docked disorder:
Wave-wanderer, beachcomber, far-flung
Singer with a shell for Nausicaa, at home
Nowhere and everywhere, but here and now,
And straddling the border once again.

Conor O'Callaghan

Three Six Five Zero

I called up tech and got the voicemail code.
It's taken me this long to find my feet.
Since last we spoke that evening it has snowed.

Fifty-four new messages. Most are old
and blinking into a future months complete.
I contacted tech to get my voicemail code

to hear your voice, not some bozo on the road
the week of Thanksgiving dubbing me his sweet
and breaking up and bleating how it snowed

the Nashville side of Chattanooga and slowed
the beltway to a standstill. The radio said sleet.
The kid in tech sent on my voicemail code.

I blew a night on lightening the system's load,
woke to white enveloping the trees, the street
that's blanked out by my leaving. It had snowed.

Lately others' pasts will turn me cold.
I heard out every message, pressed delete.
I'd happily forget my voice, the mail, its code.
We spoke at last that evening. Then it snowed.

Mary Oliver

VISITING THE GRAVEYARD

When I think of death
it is a bright enough city,
and every year more faces there
are familiar

but not a single one
notices me,
though I long for it,
and when they talk together,

which they do
very quietly,
it's in an unknowable language –
I can catch the tone

but understand not a single word –
and when I open my eyes
there's the mysterious field, the beautiful trees.
There are the stones.

Alice Oswald

Bargeman's Cabbage

Bargeman himself
Has a large hard head.
All day and night
Mostly he thinks of heaviness.
His stoop is rusted up
From pushing and hoisting.
And that's OK
That's all good business.

But Bargeman's Cabbage
She has her bare brown toes.
She has her cleavage.
She holds herself compact and cool.
All day and night
Mostly she paints the buckets.
She puts her feet up on the rail.
She can't be budged.
No, she's not coal.

Bargeman himself
Is murky, slow-spoken.
He does the slops.
He mops the kitchen.
His mouth is all mushed in
From saying nothing.
And that's OK
That's his profession.

But Bargeman's Cabbage,
No, she's not haulage.
All day and night
She paints black flowers.
She clips her nails –

A little fleet of trimmings in the canal.
She gets depressed by mud-banks.
But won't be put ashore. No, she's not planks.

She smells of blight.
It's in her clothes.
Won't be long now.
Her hands are very white.
She sits up late.
Her heart is damp
And tightly closed.
She leans as if she's listening but
Who knows?

Andrew Philip

SUMMA

Even the stones cry out.

Even the trees shrapnelled
into leaf and blossom.

Even the cough of dust
shuffling down a blade of sun.

Even the sunlight itself,
the movement of the air,

the gashed and mounded earth.
Even the tripwire heat,

even the hirpled season's
unseasonable crops;

even the implacable greenness
of each field, lawn and brae.

Even this caged
and blootered heart

rattling the bars for freedom –
even it is party

to the gathering cause.

Ann Pilling

BREASTS

They have done the state some service and they know it
suckled my boys, pleasured my man,
now they have to go under the knife.

I'm being good to them I've bought
fine cottons pricked with little flowers,
I bathe them in sweet oils and I no longer
sit like a hunchback cramming them from sight.

Why in my fat-girl days did I wear bags
to hide their lovely roundness? Why did I
mound them with cushions on our old settee?

In water they float out like lily pads
nippled with dark pink buds as this old river
creeps silently to its weir. Sad I've denied them, sad
how love, released, runs wild when it is too late.

Andrea Porter

ASSASSINATIONS

JOHN F. KENNEDY *d.*1963

I was sitting crosslegged in my grey school skirt
in front of Josie Hibbert's tiny Bakelite TV.
Upstairs her Mum was dying of something quiet.
We ran upstairs to tell her and she cried.

MARTIN LUTHER KING *d.*1968

I was with a black haired boy called Dave,
in his room still decorated with Noddy wallpaper.
Downstairs his Mum cooked egg and chips
in a long sleeved blouse to hide the bruises.

STEPHEN BANTU BIKO *d.*1977

I was walking through the Arndale Centre.
A TV called to me from a shop window.
Two stores up a shabby man was shouting.
Security was there telling him to move on.

JOHN LENNON *d.*1980

I was sitting at a green Formica table.
Across from me a girl was smoking roll ups.
She'd gouged zigzags into both her arms.
We drank tea as she picked at the scabs.

Sheenagh Pugh

ABSENT

They're everywhere, the absent. You go
out walking and see a young man
with the slight stoop and long, loping stride
of the very tall, and you have almost hailed
your son before you know it is some stranger,
some other son whose doppelganger, no doubt,
is duping his mother on a distant street.

And in the supermarket aisle you slow
to a near-stop, following old men
whose heads are mottled, whose white hair strays,
shining, on their collars, and none of them
is your father, though when one stumbles,
your hands steady him in the same moment,
as if they had been always in readiness.

You used to think death made a difference:
your mother, no longer censuring on the phone
or face to face, has long been missing
even from your dreams, nor do you meet her
drifting down some street she never saw.
Yet she too waits in ambush, in shop glass
or a sudden mirror, there before you know it.

Jeremy Reed

BLAKE

Part of the William genome
the Soho psycho's
visionary phenotype

he bounced a Boeing off computer
over the Virgin megastore
nose cone doing mock terrorist

pointers to 9/11 towers
through a turbo corridor,
roof-topped it over Oxford Street

blowing out windows from the roar,
a kamikaze coke-head
shaving the city obelisks

in a kerosene cyclone
afterburn to Heathrow.
Was handcuffed on arrival

hallucinating terminals
as mortuaries, a jackal
ripping open body bags

for diamonds at the jugular...
Diagnosed delusional
Blake bought a decommissioned jet,

lived in it on Wandsworth flats,
grew gardenias in the cockpit,
manufactured LSD

and watched incoming airliners
morph into jewel-finned jellyfish,
his girlfriend atomize on touch

into 3D molecules
and knew he'd fly again, steal a Jumbo
and kill it over Whitehall.

Kate Rhodes

The Family Visit

You brought me to this place
when we were still afraid to go anywhere
without touching – especially here,
Scots pines denying the light,
patches of bluebells refusing to be cowed.

You showed me where you used to play
inside a hollow oak, hidden behind monuments.
This was your starting point,
the ivy tangling fenland dynasties
keeping you in your place.

Your sister's here already;
dead in her teens she's been praying
a long time for a visit from you.
Her headstone lists backwards
as if she hopes someone might catch her.

Your mother and father
are so close they're almost touching,
respectable in grey marble,
holding their peace, for all the world
as if they had never hurt anyone.

Frederick Seidel

Violin

I often go to bed with a book
And immediately turn out the light.
I wake in the morning and brush and dress and go to the desk
and write.
I always put my arm in the right sleeve before I slip into the left.
I always put on my left shoe first and then I put on the right.

I happen right now
To be walking the dogs in the dangerous park at night,
Which is dangerous, which I do not like,
But I am delighted, my dog walk is a delight.
I am right-handed but mostly I am not thinking.

(CHORUS)
A man can go to sleep one night and never wake up that he knows of.
A man can walk down a Baghdad street and never walk another drop.
A man can be at his publisher's and drop dead on the way to the men's
room.
A poet can develop frontotemporal dementia.
A flavorful man can, and then he is not.

The call girls who came to our separate rooms were actually lovely.
Weren't they shocked that their customers were so illegally young?
Mine gently asked me what I wanted to do. Sin is Behovely.
Just then the phone rang –
Her friend checking if she was safe with the young Rambo,
Rimbaud.

I am pursuing you, life, to the ends of the earth across a Sahara of
tablecloth.
I look around the restaurant for breath.
I stuff my ears to sail past the siren song of the rocks.
The violin of your eyes
Is listening gently.

Peter Sirr

THE DIFFERENT RAINS COME DOWN

For motto the darting snipe
the curlew, the tree house
to which every morning I climb
bearing with aplomb
a flask of coffee, last night's line.

*

Deep in the hut the silence
roots. Days here. How long?
The meadow sings all day.
Reed-song, the lake spreads its music.

*

Yesterday
travelling though the country again
in the old jalopy, down the little roads
with only the graveyards signed
the dead handing us on
from townland to townland
until we found the junction

*

I lift the binoculars, move for a field
the sun has fallen on, has
fallen for, and soaked with light
in the middle a tree
like everyone's memory

*

Mist this morning
the hedges webbed with dew.

  *

September breakfast:
a mouthful of blackberries in the lane.

  *

I lift the binoculars: intimacies
of trees and cattle

sudden drift of smoke
sudden flitting on a wire
sudden roof
bats, suddenly,
like too fast films

suddenscape

  *

Crex crex
in the callows
the corncrake survives
to be counted by the Corncrake Officer
is it not all
I could ever have wanted

  *

The lake lies half hidden
at the end of the meadow, sending out
its reed legions
to sway drunkenly as they struggle
with the burden of the water

*

On the days he's not there
I tramp to my friend's house on the hill
and make coffee in his kitchen, I drink
from his mug, look out from his window
down towards the grey splash of the lake.
Still there, my mute swans, my life!
My friend sweats in the city
or has crept into my hut to drink from my mug
and train my binoculars on the gap between the trees
into his own distant life

*

The different rains come down
differently orchestrated
configurations of the rain
on corrugated iron
winter music, summer song
small surprise
of the secondary rain of trees
an after rain
bestowed like a gift
as you enter the canopy

*

Whatever you were
you scared the dog
and made him whimper

welcome or warning
your eyes shone
at the edge of the light

and the signs were all there

that absolute dark
the sound you made

as you ran down the road
almost colliding with us
before slipping into the field

or you were nothing
neither curse nor blessing
you were

yourself purely, your eyes blazing
caught in the porch glow
where you circled behind us

to take us in. Cold-eyed
briefly curious
and quickly gone

you left behind
a living dark, the black road
suddenly crowded

and the night filling like a corridor
all of us are passing through
with hardly a breath

between us…

                    *

Standing outside in the evening quiet
avid for light, for how the trees collect it,
disburse it, how the lower branches shine
with a colour combed out of the lake
and washed with reeds

listening to the sound a place makes
flittings and undersongs stitched into the air,
the creaturely silence, things
shifting and loosening,
a wren now from the eaves

darting to grass, then hesitating back;
standing at the edge of it as if to inhabit
some part of the conversation,
but just the way a hesitation inhabits a language,
no wren codes, deciphered trees

but standing there like nothing at all,
a post brushed by moth-wings,
a stillness rent with little cries,
a body thinned to bone like a hook
the mind might throw its hat on and forget.

Pauline Stainer

AFTERLIGHT
(for my daughter)

I chose the liquidambar tree
knowing it would light
its own dying,
like those wasted children
wrapped in gold foil
to keep them warm.

Each autumn
when leaves fall
with the first frost
not even the kings of Persia
wore such saffron-yellow shoes
across the glimmering fallow.

I use them –
the colours of grief,
like the mirror
in the cat's eye
to throw back
the single topaz at your throat.

Ruth Stone

THE FOLLIES OF MY YOUTH

It's taken me eighty-five years
to become mediocre.
How brilliant I was;
how I threw it away like used Kleenex.
I never walked the side streets of New York,
I never played tennis,
I never swam in the Olympic pool –
I know my boundaries.

My neighbor's daughter
married into the Hogg Drugstore
and died of uterine cancer at thirty.
What was all that for?
At a party given by this new rich family
I ignored my partner, the short brother.
The short brother and the tall brother
were twins. I wanted to dance with the tall one.
The short one went inside and cried.
His mother made cruel remarks about me.

Could I have done the same as the neighbor's daughter,
married the short Hogg brother, and died young, too?
Here I am, old and poor.
Where is that short twin now?
Where is his loyal mother?
But I didn't think of bettering myself;
there were too many books in the world.
There was so much I wanted to read.

Tess Taylor

ALTOGETHER ELSEWHERE

They multiply, these cities of the heart.
Rooms we stop to rest our bodies in.

Brief beds: One California night
I saw humpbacked coastal ranges,

and scotch-tinged, wet from naked swimming,
woke to smokestacks and dawn in Queens.

Light split the branches of new trees.
Stage-set lives implied themselves from props.

Now morning, with its birds, construction sites,
sun on a western freeway, city garden filled

with lavender, with childhood light
this midsummer too will go soon.

O unfinishable rooms,
homes that feel so real so briefly,

I feel you incomplete me, incompletely.

Arto Vaun

They have never been on a ship before, let alone
Anything called *sea* – 1947
And Beirut is, like them, dumb about the dense future
Already attaching itself like a cataract

Just passengers and waves – a little girl's hand
Slipping in and out of her eighteen-year-old mother's

Two hands, the world on that boarding plank
The sound of shuffling feet in some kind of counterpoint
With the echo of water and the dry swallow in throats

Partial moon sheds what it can – father and grandfather
Talk little, feel their ribcages are lit from the inside

Having made this decision and now, stepping off land,
One or both of them sense control spinning away
Like an angel tired of having to watch

The boarding plank bends from the future, arms
Clutching arms clutching whatever they can carry
Voices consumed by the in-between place, a small crevice –
Even in the most tenuous hand-holding there is
Still more warmth than the most glaring sun
                         About to come

Everyone sits where they can as though at mass
And the off-white ship begins to creak like a song
                         No one has heard before

Mark Waldron

THE BEARS ARE SKIING THROUGH THE TREES

Shush, *shush*, go the skis in the snow.
Oh, the concentrated glee across their furred faces!

Oh, oh, slicing that way! Oh, and slicing this!
Wanton smiles among the berries

and the honey in their stomachs.
Smiles like tiny, gravid bombs.

Chipmunks (which also should be hibernating)
watch from woody holes and wish

they had the wherewithal to clap their leather paws,
to holler piping hot and minute winter whoops!

Oh, how strange to find you here, touching your mouth
with icy fingers, the world's true cold on you.

William Wall

Job in Heathrow

I

with the frightened crowd
for whom every new alarum
is an authority
queuing in drifts
between levels
the so-called waiting lounges
of the so-called world

the word is out
there are bombs
in the whiskey
no carry on
this is the last straw

& nervous people
& nervous men in stab vests
& nervous men in puffa jackets
& no smoking signs
& this is a silent airport
you pay the man
& you wait for a sign
there the prisoners rest together
the small and great are there
studying departures
in a state of heightened alert
code somewhere close to titian

a man holds his woman in his arms
& another watches the door expectantly
& the enemy comes on his own feet
to his grave

we are a trifle unsettled

we think about sodoku & the crossword
as though minding minutiae
the universe will look after itself
this is the world as it is *habibi*
it's all we know
try to step off
& the man will bring you down

2

master I cried
who are these bastards
do we have any idea who these people are
willowy women in Gucci shoes
men in silk leather jackets
they circulate freely
in the recycled air
must we do homage
or will a simple nod be enough
a greeting *ex gratia*
do they expect to be questioned
to assist enquiries
interrogation
water-boarding even
look here comes one crying
hopeless hopeless hopeless
& are we supposed to sympathise
when the gentry find themselves in the
same boat
or plane
as everyone else
or at least in the same lounge
love brought her down she says
according to her biography
it was a chance encounter at a drug-fuelled

orgy
in somebody somebody's motor yacht
the coke blew her away
blew her brains away
& opened her legs
& wore her sinovial membrane down
it all sounds a little hollow now
with the end of the world upon us
& bombs in the whiskey
love love love she says
so much for all you need is love

3

they come & go like cranes
restless creatures look
& their pale limbs against the azure sky

I see myself in you
a sly oriental craft
sails on the water

& are we supposed to sympathise
& who are these people
extra-communitari

there in the upper circle
the automatic doors
are automatic from the outside only

we see them as it were through a tinted
glass
wringing their hands
begging admission

these troublesome ghosts
what was it Marx said in the famous

opening
something haunting

a man had his left hand chopped off
for with it he slew his master
& he begged a pipe of tobacco

& then he died
the ultimate manumission
in those days they knew their place

he was a slave & his place of execution
is here
upon this fatal shore or landing

at least Virginia apologised
they come & go like cranes
restless creatures look

& they make their homes in marsh &
useless ground
& leave when they can
those Turks Hector & Heraclites

& Euclid the Egyptian
Pythagoras the fundamentalist
& all the gang

Avicenna the metaphysician
thinking about his credentials
they don't let Uzbekistanis operate on
Christians

even in Hell
someone is tuning up
old Ali Farka Touré on the air guitar

a session
come on boys
when did you make a run for it

no running here
cancer of the bones
death comes like ice

the heart of the moon
where you come from they get that
on a bad day as I remember

4

& somebody says the loo is blocked
dear god
what will they think of next
they've closed off the last line of escape
another safety valve
what will become of us

my father gave me Marcus Aurelius
on the last day of my holidays
& the old emperor stood me in good
stead you know
communing with himself

at Gallipoli
we ran our ship ashore into the sand
we saw tesserae in the parados
& I said to my sub I said

six or seven thousand years of this
& here we are again attacking the Turks
will it never end
meaning we the philhellenes

& that idiot Bean
is that a light I see on Tenedos
I'm dying for a smoke dear boy
& I'm too old for this

a decent education makes it all worthwhile
knowing what we know et cetera
this one is a beauty
see how he walks

don't you love an Arab
oh the Sheik of Araby
if I don't take a leak
I shall leak

& my sub said to me
an ignorant child
it's all this Allah business sir
that gets to me

5

that girl bled to death
a million tiny wounds
& everyone said how well she looked
jammed against the partition
her pants still around her knees
a note of caution
peace accursed woolf
or words to that effect
they would not give her the last rites
the blacksuit serpents
mal dare e mal tener
they look after their own
but she is a beauty no mistake
they eat each other
round & round they go

her state is blessed
out of this world at least
poor child
they direct the almighty guns
against self-harmers
she was my daughter
your daughter too

6

the guards wear sunglasses
a society of spectacles as the man said
like the dark ground of a cameo
except in reverse
their faces are blanked by their eyes
if someone farts we're dead
see their trigger fingers
& the somnolent insouciance
of the human face
if we had an air force
we would send you bombers

for I do not know whose voice is crying
when I cry
never look back at the border
the furies follow behind
never poke fire with a knife
never piss into the sun
abstain from beans
these few precepts mark you well
what of the isles of the blest
not for us my son
not our kind

they look at us
& we look at them
there's bush that vicious mole

another non-statement
of what he thinks
another good one about axes
or the coalition of the willing
not the coerced
do we have to have TV everywhere
fly sky news news sky fly
o for a universal remote

please note the automatic doors
are no longer automatic
access to the open areas is restricted
arrivals is closed
all unattended baggage will be destroyed
nervous people
will be arrested
please note
the contrapuntal strains
of childhood & exile
we are all strangers in one sense or
another
depending on each other

7

our children are hungry
they look up
& are not fed
not even a complimentary coke
the cost of living
higher than expected
year on year increases
sometimes out of reach
never easy to make ends meet
but what can you do
the grey wolf
walks the steppes of the heart

every father
every mother
knows the sound of his passing
his fierce eyes
but one day you must let go
you just let go

8

I said you should eat your garlic
it's good for digestion
& indicated in these cases
but you made a pig of yourself
friend Elpenor
you were pissed
when you fell from that roof
a troublesome shade
don't you look at me like that

out on that headland
the wind whistling in our drawers
remember the fire we burned
you kindled up quick enough
bare flesh & bread & young dark wine
once is enough for anyone
once & for all
but I did it twice
that was the kind I was
until the going down of the sun
when all the ways grew dark
& the sea was dark
& dark-prowed ships moved on it
let go let go I said
& we pulled out of that place
on our travels
what fun we had
at the mercy of the wind

wherever our fancy took us

we querulous ghosts

this is our ancient future
this holding bay
this waiting room
where no room awaits
this offing
this roadstead
this glass hole in the horizon
we could be flying
& instead we're falling
out of the world & into the air
life is ticketless
point to point
& then there is Costa Coffee
& fear

9

how do you feel my dear
stricken at heart
but you're on television
smile
I am stricken at heart
& losing the sight of my eyes
no flocks of sheep nor ploughed-land
saw I
but a barren wilderness
I am stricken at heart
o desolate men
let us hide our faces
sighing & whispering
in this place of tears
nor law nor council
but everyone in his own place
alone

there was abundant flesh
& so called consumer durables
& we looked at the sun's single eye
& saw the travel brochure
& thought why not
it was a hole

promiscuous death
no rights knows
never tell them your real name
say I am no one or someone
anyone
but who I am

that man is a renowned poet
see his hair
the thinking man's easy answer
impounded
in this nether crib
after Adorno said that business about
poetry
how can the man dare
never mind this or that holocaust
I say
better yet
think about holocausts
as something people did
a long time ago
& are inclined to do
once in a while
take the long view
politics makes you strident
which is bad news for the poet
whatever way you think about it

silence
is the only answer
& nothing comes of that
so twitter on
fiddle even
at least we're occupied

11

& for his simple heart
I loved him
three days he was dying
it was past all tragedy
& we were eating & drinking
like there was no tomorrow
sorrow takes you that way
rain cleared after midnight
& the tide came in
all the small sounds
of the drowning foreshore
sea-creatures coming home
& land-creatures fleeing
& he drowned I suppose
it certainly sounded like that
a man who looked out on the sea
all his life
but a landsman really
not overly privileged by death

12

I look up & there is glass
or maybe sky
summer clouds
brittle & bare
& I think Mr Death how do you do
this bubble of blue
when the sky falls

all we ask for is plausible deniability
our travelling companions
our ancient kinship
consanguinity

I will deny everything three times
how we die matters less than why
or so they say
but if there is an easy way out

13

we are inclined to confidences
as the light fades
& calling to mind the distant past
& places we will never see again
departures are cancelled
someone says
when they let us smoke it's the end
& pret-a-manger is running out
but we never despair
which is how we won the war

the game involves numbers
& knowing their place
the so-called biometric data
we're looking for coherence
not meaning
competing against ourselves

we sense
things coming together
a great clandestine gathering
something that happens elsewhere

anything to keep the nights at bay
I get anxiety

a heightened state of alert
xanax is what I get
we're just fading aren't we
we're looking at the twilight
oh yes
fading

Sue Wood

The Woman Who Refused to Move

We measured the distance between
the cliff edge and our land.
He took the tape, my dress-making tape
coiled like an ammonite
tight in the tea cup.

He came back up the path
fingers holding
this measure of earth-shift
gave it to me as if distance
was a precious thing.

Lilies, roses and sweet sea lavender
slipped between shifting sands
then our terrace wall
and on the turncoat tide, our bean row
looped in coral and green.

Today he held my hand
palm uppermost
tracing the lines to their sea-fog endings.

On the house wall
a split like hackles rising.

Publisher acknowledgements

Lucy M Alford · OYSTERS · *Warwick Review*

Zeeba Ansari · MARRIAGE INTERVIEW · *The Frogmore Papers*

Ros Barber · MATERIAL · *Material* · Anvil

Peter Bennet · THE SQUIRREL · *The Glass Swarm* · Flambard Press

Paul Blake · TRIBOLUMINESCENCE · *Brittle Star*

John Burnside · POPPY DAY · *The Hunt in the Forest* · Jonathan Cape

Vahni Capildeo · FROM FIRST TO LAST HIS BOOKS, THAT STARTED
THIN, GREW LESS, AND I'D PUT MYSELF IN DEBT TO BUY ALL FOUR
OR FIVE OF THEM · *Undraining Sea* · Egg Box

Ciaran Carson · IN RUINS · *On the Night Watch* · Gallery Books

Anne Carson · WILDLY CONSTANT · *London Review of Books*

Billy Collins · AUBADE · *Ballistics* · Picador

Stewart Conn · CONUNDRUM · *The Frogmore Papers*

David Constantine · FRIEZE · *Nine Fathom Deep* · Bloodaxe

John F Deane · STRANGER · *A Little Book of Hours* · Carcanet

Jane Draycott · THE SQUARE · *Over* · Carcanet – Oxford Poets

Joe Duggan · POET OF THE TROUBLES · *Fizzbombs* · tall-lighthouse

Antony Dunn · LOVE POETRY · *Bugs* · Carcanet – Oxford Poets

Simon Z East · CASE NOTES: STRATHCLYDE POLICE STATION ·
The Erotic Review

Carrie Etter · THE TRAPEZE ARTIST'S DEAR JOHN LETTER ·
The Tethers · Seren

Katy Evans-Bush · TO MY NEXT LOVER · *Me and the Dead* · Salt

Paul Farley · MOLES · *Poetry Review*

Keri Finlayson · THE JAZZ SINGER · *Rooms* · Shearsman Books

Mark Ford · HOURGLASS · *Times Literary Supplement*

Jacqueline Gabbitas · HARNESSING THE POWER OF GRASS ·
Staple New Writing

Sam Gardiner · THE BEAUTY OF THE BUTTONS · *The Frogmore Papers*

Vona Groake · BODKIN · *Spindrift* · The Gallery Press

Chris Hardy · DEFINITELY HUMAN · *The Journal*

Kevin Hart · THAT LIFE · *Young Rain* · Bloodaxe

John Hartley Williams · CAFÉ·DES ARTISTES · *Café des Artistes* ·
Jonathan Cape

Oli Hazzard · MOVING IN · *PN Review*

Stanley Moss · Autumn · *Rejoicing* · Anvil

Andrew Motion · From the Journal of a Disappointed Man · *The Cinder Path* · Faber and Faber

Christopher North · Taino · *Brittle Star*

Sean O'Brien · The Landing-Stage · *Times Literary Supplement*

Conor O'Callaghan · Three Six Five Zero · Bridport Prize

Meghan O'Rourke · Descent · Palimpsest · *Halflife* · W W Norton

Sharon Olds · Self Exam · Diagnosis · *One Secret Thing* · Jonathan Cape

Mary Oliver · Visiting the Graveyard · *Red Bird* · Bloodaxe

Alice Oswald · Bargeman's Cabbage · *Weeds and Wild Flowers* · Faber and Faber

Don Paterson · The Lie · Rain · *Rain* · Faber and Faber

Andrew Philip · Summa · *The Ambulance Box* · Salt

Ann Pilling · Breasts · *Home Field* · Arrowhead Press

Peter Porter · No Heaven Cold Enough · Shakespeare's Defeat · *Better than God* · Picador

Andrea Porter · Assassinations · *A Season of Small Insanities* · Salt

Sheenagh Pugh · Absent · *Long-Haul Travellers* · Seren

Jeremy Reed · Blake · *West End Survival Kit* · Waterloo Press

Christopher Reid · A Scattering · Afterlife · *A Scattering* · Areté Books

Kate Rhodes · The Family Visit · *The Alice Trap* · Enitharmon

Robin Robertson · At Roane Head · *London Review of Books*

Frederick Seidel · Violin · *Ooga-Booga* · Faber and Faber

Peter Sirr · The Different Rains Come Down · *Irish Pages*

Elizabeth Speller · Finistère · Bridport Prize

Pauline Stainer · Afterlight · *Crossing the Snowline* · Bloodaxe

Ruth Stone · The Follies of My Youth · *What Love Comes To New & Selected Poems* · Bloodaxe

George Szirtes · Song · *The Liberal*

Tess Taylor · Altogether Elsewhere · *Warwick Review*

Arto Vaun · xlvii · *Capillarity* · Carcanet

Mark Waldron · The Bears Are Skiing Through the Trees · *The Brand New Dark* · Salt

William Wall · Job in Heathrow · *The Shop*

Hugo Williams · Poems to My Mother · *West End Final* · Faber and Faber

C K Williams · EITHER / OR · *Poetry Review*
Sue Wood · THE WOMAN WHO REFUSED TO MOVE · *Imagine Yourself*
to be Water · Cinnamon Press